A Daughter's Memoir of Hope
Through Cancer, Caregiving, and Grief

Faith
and a Tube of
Lipstick

MARLA LACKEY

ISBN: 978-1-7358477-0-2 (softcover)
ISBN: 978-1-7358477-1-9 (ebook)
Library of Congress Control Number: 2020921575

Published by Marla Lackey

Cover design by Jennifer Burrell
Interior design and ebook by Jill Ronsley, suneditwrite.com

Printed and bound in the USA

To my beloved mother,
Sandra Lozano,
in gratitude for all the ways she shared
her love and faith with me,
both here on earth and from heaven

❧

Mom,
I love you high (kiss)
as the moon (kiss)
and the stars (kiss)
and the sun (kiss)
and the sky. (kiss)

Contents

Introduction

It was the spring of 2006 when my mom was diagnosed with breast cancer. I wasn't ready. At that time, I was in my late thirties, struggling to balance on the tightrope of life as a nurse, a wife, and a mother of four small children. It's hard to believe that during that same season of my life, I had already taken on the role of co-caregiver alongside my mom for my dad, who had battled an aggressive form of bladder cancer.

I was in no shape to divide any of my fears, attention, and prayers away from my life as I knew it. This was my *mom,* for heaven's sake. She was my first best friend. My rock. My confidante and my prayer warrior. I was scared to death about the unknown. I feared not just her prognosis, but how a mommy's girl like me, who had been attached to this woman's soul since birth, would be able to handle the pain of seeing my *world* struggle and fight for her life.

But as usual, God had my back. Throughout my mother's four-year battle, God provided me with not just His usual blessings of strength, comfort, and peace (which, of course, I welcomed with open arms), but also totally unexpected ones. He provided me with the ability to see and feel the power behind full-circle moments and numerous spiritual revelations, allowing me to find—even during the most agonizing points in my journey—sacredness, beauty, and joy in being my mom's primary caregiver.

What I mean by *full-circle moments* is that everything my mom taught me growing up is what I ended up teaching her right back. I'm not just talking about the typical role reversal duties like staying up with her all night when she was sick or helping her bathe or eat. I'm talking about something entirely different.

To my surprise, I discovered both before and after my mom passed away that many of our full-circle moments had these "spiritual aha" themes that revolved around our faith in God, hard life lessons from our past and present, and yes, even a tube of lipstick. Although I didn't realize it at the time, all the spiritual lessons that kept popping up were laying a foundation for the strength I would need to get through my own living hell.

Once I was able to snap out of my grief coma long enough to speak in complete sentences (which took almost a year), I found myself wanting to tell anyone and everyone about every full-circle moment, every spiritual aha, and every heavenly sign that revolved around me and my mom. I was desperate to keep both my sanity and Mom's memory alive. Telling my stories was all I had to give.

Yet, if someone had tried to tell me during that fragile time of caregiving and grief that one day, I'd be bursting at the seams, ready to write a blog and a book (and even publicly speak about the not-so-obvious blessings that stemmed from my pain), I would've brushed them off as crazy.

Now here I am, ten years later, ready to share with you the details of how I discovered and applied the blessings that ultimately resulted in my reclaiming a spiritual connection with my mother—a connection that would live on even after her passing.

This book chronicles these experiences, each chapter starting off with a story from my innocent childhood of the seventies, turbulent teen years of the eighties, and somewhat stable young adult life during the 2000s. As you read further into each chapter, you'll see how many of my childhood experiences directly correlate to each stage of my mom's cancer journey.

I'll be honest, though: Having to relive everything all over again as I wrote took a toll on my heart, mind, and soul. Had it not been by the grace of God, my parents' heavenly guidance—especially my mom—my family's and friends' unwavering support (and shoot, even some good ol' professional counseling), you wouldn't be holding this book. And for all of that and all of them, I'm forever grateful.

Like me, there comes a time in many people's lives when they're thrust into the reality of having to care for an aging or terminally ill parent. It's a thought that many adult children like myself tend to put on the back burner in hopes of delaying the inevitable, unimaginable future. It's just too hard to fathom that our parents will suffer, decline, and depend on us in ways we're not prepared for.

So in writing my memoir, It's been my intention from the get-go to not only carry out my mom's legacy, but to help caregivers like you, who need to catch your breath and find a way to break out of the disconnected, autopilot mindset of caregiving. Who yearn to find the blessings in this painful process. I know all too well the dreadful thoughts and feelings that stir within each and every one of you as you take on the daily stresses and demands of caring for a parent.

Many times, caregivers like us sink deeper and deeper into pits of despair and wonder how in the world we'll handle any more burnout, fatigue, overwhelm, and even grief—especially if we're juggling our time and energy with our own family at home.

You may be like me and think to yourself: where is God in all this? How can I find the good during this

challenging time in my life? When there's so much suffering all around me, how am I supposed to bridge the
gap between feeling my pain and appreciating blessings?

If these concerns weigh you down on a daily basis or
keep you up at night, take heart: there is hope. Remember
that your role as an adult child caregiver is a divine assignment from God—one that you can always feel proud
of and honored by, no matter how tired, sad, and frustrated you may feel. He chose *you* to care for your dying
parent for a reason. He chose *you* to be their Earth Angel,
to serve your loved one throughout every stage of their
illness, and to help escort them back to their heavenly
home when it's time. Embrace this role with an open
heart, knowing that He will give you the strength to see
you through.

And maybe, just maybe, He chose *you* to read this
book as a tool to help you understand that behind every
life lesson with your parent (good or bad), there is *always*
richness and beauty—full-circle moments that will no
doubt rekindle the fire in your soul.

My intention is that the heartfelt stories and insights
in this memoir will offer you the support and inspiration
you need to discover your own special blessings, your
own powerful full-circle moments, and your own aha
moments—all of which are the perfect mindful ingredi-
ents to help you move forward with strength and faith
during your caregiving and grief journey.

I promise you that if God can use my experiences of faith, a simple tube of lipstick, and everything in between to see me through my heartache season, surely you can expect Him to do the same for you as He reveals your own custom made blessings.

God bless you all, dear Earth Angels.

Chapter 1

Agony of Defeat

*I*t was the Friday before spring break of 1985. I was fourteen years old, and I was convinced my world had ended. It was my own personal D-Day of Demotion, Distress, and Defeat. Little did I know that it would prepare me for the upcoming D-Day of my mother's life.

I had just completed my sophomore year on the varsity cheerleading squad and convinced my overly confident self that I'd make it onto the squad again. *No problem. Once varsity, always varsity.*

Since the seventh grade, much of my identity had revolved around being an esteemed member of the team. From that time on, I ate, slept, and bled cheer, pouring my heart and soul into every routine as if my life depended on it.

But somehow, I had missed the dang memo that cheerleading was evolving into a real sport. While other girls on the squad were advancing to more complex techniques—perfecting their back handsprings and back tucks like professional gymnasts—I remained stuck in the fluff of it all, doing the basic kick, cartwheel, and round-off over and over again. I also tried to ignore the twenty pounds I had gained, which made my jumps lower and tumbling techniques sloppier.

Inevitably, tryout day arrived, and despite my best efforts, I couldn't stay in the zone. I couldn't even hear myself think. My mind was a total blur as I searched for my self-belief through the murkiness of my panic. Just before I was about to lose it, I remembered the antidote—the one and only remedy that could always calm my nerves: Mom's voice.

Minutes before I was set to go on, I rushed through the crowded classroom toward the phone that we weren't supposed to use. But in that moment, following the rules was the least of my worries. I needed relief right away. Fortunately, she picked up on the first ring.

"I'm so nervous, Mom," I shouted over the phone before she had a chance to speak.

I could tell that she was caught off guard by my impromptu call, but in characteristic fashion, she kept her cool under the pressure of not just hearing but feeling the panic in my voice.

"Oh, honey, you're going to do great," she reassured me. "Just do your best, and make sure you pray, okay? It'll be all right."

Of course, she *would* bring up prayer. Growing up, I learned from the master herself that prayer was the cure-all for everything, including nerves. She taught me well; I always took her prayer advice seriously. How in the world could she think that I needed to be reminded to pray? Didn't she know I already had a thousand Hail Marys and another thousand Our Fathers set on replay in my head as I simmered in my pressure cooker of worry?

"I have been praying, Mom, but it's not working. What if I don't ..."

"Listen to me, young lady," she firmly interrupted. Her tone had changed in an instant, as if she were grabbing my face though the phone. "You need to slow down, take a deep breath, and ask God to help you. You hear me?"

Everything around me stopped, including my reflexive urge to make a rebellious comeback. Any time Mom started a sentence with "young lady" and ended with, "you hear me?" I knew she meant business.

As always, Mom was right. After being whisked away in a swirling tornado of my own doubt and a ceaseless repetition of prayers, I needed her strict words of wisdom to get back to basics. Without resistance, I did as she said.

In the silence that followed, I closed my eyes, took two long, deep breaths, and with the purest intention, cried out inside my heart, *Jesus, please help me.*

In the very next moment, an overwhelming sense of peace rushed through me. It was magical. As a teenager, I didn't have a lot of life experience, or the common sense

9

to identify or understand what it actually feels like to have the Holy Spirit take over your whole being. I had heard about it through Bible stories, through prayers said at church, and in Mom's off-the-cuff comments about the Holy Spirit helping her during her rough times—but never had I experienced it myself. Looking back now, I realize that the peaceful, magical feeling was indeed the Holy Spirit making an official debut in my life. And that experience would mark a full-circle moment that I would share with my Mom years down the road.

Guided by this undeniable heavenly force, the silence broke as Mom wrapped her words of comfort around me: "You'd better get going. And don't worry; I'll be praying for you. See you when you get home, Miss Varsity Cheerleader. I love you."

Trying not to smear my mascara, I fanned my face from my tears of relief. I hung up the phone, relieved by my maternal antidote with its side of Holy Spirit. Mom's positive reassurance and wit provided me with the confidence to break through my nerves of steel. Before I knew it, I was back in the zone and my original theory: *Once varsity, always varsity.*

I blinked as the proctor's voice snapped me back to reality.

"Marla! You're up next."

Suddenly, my stomach was rehearsing the cartwheels I was about to perform before a panel of shrewd judges.

Whispering one more *Hail Mary* for good measure, I headed toward the gym door.

My tennis shoes squeaked loudly against the polished wood floor as my legs trembled with each step onto the court. I was immediately struck by the stark emptiness of the stands, which would ordinarily be packed with a full audience of students, parents, and teachers. The stone-faced judges watched in silence as I began to perform my routine.

Despite the uncomfortable setting, I pulled out every ounce of charm I had in me, projecting my voice and school spirit like nobody's business. I struggled to mask the droopiness of each toe touch jump that came with my less-than-Olympic-level cartwheels and round-offs.

When my routine was finally finished, I walked off the court in a stupor.

"How'd it go? Did you remember everything?"

I stood there in shock as my Olympian cheerleader friends hovered around me. "It went good, I guess." I wondered how my nerves had made it out of that gym intact.

Internally, my confidence in my performance drowned out any doubts. But I wasn't about to toot my own horn to the public or to boast my major highlight moments (which mostly included my loud voice, undeniable spirit, and a few extra high kicks). Mom had taught me better than that. Instead, I decided to join the rest of the misery-loves-company group, confessing to my fellow drama queens that my tryout routine sucked just as much as theirs.

Somehow, sharing my misery made the three hours of torturous waiting go by faster. The results were finally in. Wired with fear, excitement, and a whole lot of sugar, we all headed to the gym and lined up by our tryout numbers.

At our school, we didn't have the results posted up on a wall for everyone to crowd around and look at. We were required to stand side by side with our hands behind our backs and our eyes closed. The judges and sponsor then walked behind us and placed a piece of construction paper shaped like a megaphone in each of our hands. Each megaphone said either "varsity" or "JV," or it was blank for those who didn't make either team.

Shaking like a runner-up in the Miss America pageant, I caressed the paper in the palm of my sweaty hand as if I could feel the word "varsity" written in braille.

Our cheer sponsor broke the tense silence with her notorious you'd-better-do-what-I-say-or-else voice. "On the count of three, you may all look at your paper."

From that moment forward, every word, every second felt like slow motion. "OOONNNEEE … TTTWWOOO … TTHRREE!"

I looked down and saw, in the boldest ink ever, the letters "JV" jump out from the paper and stab me in the heart. I kept staring at that dumb megaphone, turning it around in hopes that the word "varsity" was written on the other side.

The judges must've made a mistake. No way I've been demoted to the JV team. No way.

Shocked and confused and left to die right there on the gym floor, I was overcome with humiliation. Back then, this kind of demotion was totally unheard of. Neither my heart nor my ego could take it.

No longer varsity material, I stood in the gym and sobbed while the now All-American Olympic team whooped and hollered at their victory. Recognizing her agony just a few feet away, I knew my good friend, Yvette had been demoted too. After a failed attempt to console each other, we agreed to meet at my house

Tears of defeat clouded my vision on the drive home. The dreadful thought of having to tell Mom made me cry even harder. *My poor Mom. This is going to crush her—I know it. I hate it when she cries.*

Mom and I always had a way of absorbing each other's pain. It was what we had done from the time I was a little girl. And we did it well.

Her mood dropped ten levels any time I was sick, hurt by a friend, or just dealing with the highs and lows of PMS. She would morph into a version of me in no time flat. In the beginning, I felt comforted and understood by her infusion with my soul, but later it got to me. I couldn't take it.

"Please don't worry, Momma. I'll be okay," I'd say, while patting her arm. And like clockwork, she'd absorb my angst and turn it right back around.

"I'm all right. Now, don't you worry about me either." We would sit there, patting each other until the other perked up enough to stop the madness of our deep connection.

As soon as I reached the house, Mom opened the front door to greet her "Miss Varsity Cheerleader!" Her eyes, full of wonder and excitement, met mine, but before she could say a word, I cried out from my gut. "I didn't make it, Mom! I didn't make it. I got demoted to JV." I fell in her open arms and bawled like a baby.

I'm not sure what made my mother cry more—the news of my demotion or the fact that she physically had to hold me up to keep me from falling to the floor.

Even though I was almost as tall as she was, Mom's stature seemed huge in that moment. Her petite arms felt strong as she cradled my dead weight. All it took to loosen the grip of my despair was her slight swaying back and forth. Then, both of us became calm enough to speak in complete sentences.

Holding back tears, while dazed and confused, she directly asked, "What happened? Did you forget the routine? Did you fall down? What?"

"No, Mom. Everything went fine. I thought I did good."

As I spewed out the details of my mediocre tryout performance, it dawned on me that maybe my definition of good wasn't good enough. I'm sure in the back of my mother's mind, she thought the same thing. But neither of us would admit that our "once varsity, always varsity" mentality had backfired on us.

After a few minutes, Yvette and her mother arrived, and we sat at the dining room table. Mother Bear Mode kicked as both of them strategized how to right this terrible wrong. "I'll go by the school office next Monday and ask to see the scorecard," Mom blurted out. "Don't worry. We'll get this straightened out."

Her firm tone of support barely scratched the surface of my pain, though. My heart was bitter. I had failed. So *much for the prayers, God. They didn't even work. No way, no how am I going back to the JV squad.* Another wave of dramatic adolescent tears flowed. *I can't believe this is happening. No! No! No!*

Out of pure desperation, I convinced my dramatic teenage self to listen to every single word Mom said—even if I didn't yet believe that I was going to be okay and that God was going to take care of me. Holding my faith from that moment of peace I was given by the Holy Spirit was, as all human beings have discovered, a difficult task. Still, it helped me immensely when I was faced with a much steeper challenge more than twenty years later.

15

"No! No! I can't do this! I can't!"

Mom's frantic cry echoed through the half-empty parking lot as we stood beside my car. The fear in her voice pierced my broken heart. The two of us had just received the devastating news: breast cancer.

It was the spring of 2006, long after my adolescent cheerleading defeat. I was now thirty-seven, and Mom was only sixty-two years old. Too young to encounter such a D-Day of Diagnosis, Defeat, and Distress.

As she started to have a panic attack, I tried to take control of the situation, coaching her with the go-to breathing techniques I had learned as a labor and delivery nurse. "Just breathe, Mom. In through your nose and out through your mouth like this."

I could tell that she was increasingly losing control. Unable to focus, she was inconsolable. My mother was falling to pieces, and there wasn't a thing I could do about it.

Our lifelong tendency of absorbing each other's pain resurfaced to the nth degree. I wished I could trade places with her, that I could be the one falling apart, collapsing into her protective arms just like the night of my varsity fail. But it was imperative that I stay strong and calm.

Strangely, a silly slapping scene from the old sitcom, *Laverne & Shirley*, came to mind. As I pictured the two women smacking one another, I wished something that simple could bring Mom back under control. It was a ridiculous thought, but it helped me momentarily detach from the intensity of the moment. Instead of resorting to slapstick humor, I held her petite body tight in my arms and calmed her with quiet shushing sounds. The gentle rocking mimicked how she had soothed me as a child—and later, how she soothed her grandchildren.

It worked for Mom, too, but there was no doubt that it was from more than the rocking and the shushing—the Holy Spirit was clearly present. I recognized it from that moment when I was a teenager. Time stood still and was peaceful, giving us a chance to catch our breath in unison.

With both of us fully present and rational, Mom's beautiful hazel eyes met mine. I noticed right away that she was now looking *at* me instead of *through* me. Gently and softly, I said, "You're right, Mom. You can't do this alone, but with God, you *can*. He does not intend for you to do this all by yourself." I paused, smiling. "Remember your favorite scripture: 'I can do all things through Christ who strengthens me.' Mom, it's time to *apply* and *live* what you've always believed."

Her demeanor became even more peaceful as I stood there, in awe of the words I had spoken because I knew they weren't my own.

"You're right, honey. You're right. I'm just so scared."

"I know, Momma. It's going to be okay," I assured her as the two of us hugged, sealing the deal that we were both on the same page with our new and improved belief-fueled optimism.

Once in the car, we wiped our eyes and blew our clogged noses. Mom flipped down the sun visor and peered in the mirror as she rubbed away her smudged mascara and blended the tear stains into what was left of her makeup.

Within a split second, I wanted to cry all over again—but for entirely different reasons. I was comforted by the sight of my mother searching her purse for her lipstick. In her true ready-to-kick-cancer's-ass kind of way, she applied her favorite pink Revlon, smacked her lips, and said, "Let's get a Frosty at Wendy's and then head over to St. Matthew Chapel, okay?"

I couldn't believe my ears. Without hesitation, she whipped out her wallet and started to count her wadded up dollar bills—a ritual she always completed before going out to eat.

Oh my God, look at this! I thought. I couldn't get over the fact that just minutes earlier, she had been drenched in fear, clinging to me for dear life. And now, here she was, back to the take-charge mom I knew who always insisted on paying for my meals, even now that I was an adult.

For a split second, I questioned whether denial was the reason for her quick turnover—but I knew deep down it wasn't. This was real. This was Mom. This was God.

I was so relieved and proud to see her behaving like her usual self, breaking out her go-to stress remedies of lipstick, a sweet treat, and her faith to get through her D-Day. I wanted to stick my head out of the car sun roof and shout, "Did you hear that, world? She wants to get a Frosty and go to the chapel! Woo-hoo!"

After collecting our chocolate ice cream treats, we sat at a table in the nearly empty Wendy's dining area. Thankfully, nobody was around just in case one of us started crying again. We rehashed the unexpected diagnosis and strategized the best way to tell our family. I know now that the Holy Spirit was still at work; how else could we have avoided breaking down all over again at the mere thought of their devastated reactions?

In the end, we decided I would tell my older siblings, Mark and Monica, and Mom would tell Dad and her sisters once she got home.

"Everyone is going to be so upset," Mom said softly, as the tears began again.

Validating her tears with my own, I held her hands from across the table.

As a family, it felt like our world was truly falling apart. Unbelievably, a year earlier, Dad had been diagnosed with bladder cancer and was currently undergoing chemotherapy. I couldn't process the thought that both of my parents would be bald, sick, and fighting for their lives at the same time. It was bad enough to watch Dad go through cancer's chokehold. Now, I had to watch Mom endure the same struggle.

By the time we drove into the parking lot at St. Matthew's, part of me was worried. How would I keep myself from causing a scene once I stepped inside the chapel? I was feeling so fragile that I wasn't sure I could stay in control. But thanks to the presence of the Holy Spirit, I did.

The familiar stained glass windows and statues inside the chapel were comforting. It was our safe haven—our home base in the midst of the chaos. As we normally did, Mom and I entered the front pew and knelt before the altar. Looking up at the statue of Jesus, I was so comforted by the lifelike appearance of his light brown eyes and kind, chiseled face that it calmed me down enough to keep from yelling out, "Jesus, help us!"

Immediately, I began to have an internal dialogue with the One who could rescue me from my pain and heal my parents.

In God's presence, Mom and I were overwhelmed with love and strength as our hands clasped at heart level while our tears flowed like liquid prayers. Conscious of others around us, however, we kept our cries muffled and wiped our tears away before they formed a puddle on the floor.

After praying, the two of us walked over to the side of the chapel and each lit a candle as a final plea for healing. Mom's dewy face glowed under the soft light of the candles' flickering flames. She radiated a kind of beauty I had never seen before. She had always been physically attractive with her blonde hair and delicate features, but what I saw that day was something different. I saw the beauty of her strong inner warrior shine through. Her obvious serenity reflected what my heart sought, and I knew God would see us both through.

Feeling renewed, we left the church, arm in arm. As we headed home, I was surprised that after all the tears that had been shed in that chapel, Mom didn't once look in the mirror or reapply her makeup. But she didn't need to; her faith had been restored. And so had mine.

Although I didn't have the words to describe it at that time, I recognize now that the mental process I used to survive those moments of anxiety was a form of mindfulness. If you're not familiar with this concept, mindfulness is an elevated state of consciousness—a heightened awareness of our thoughts and emotions as they are experienced.

It wasn't until years later that I discovered the power of mindfulness and meditation. I realized then, however, that I had been practicing mindfulness all along without knowing it. This, along with the divine spiritual guidance I received from the Holy Spirit and from others who share my faith, is what helped me endure all of the stress, grief, anxiety, sadness, and more that were yet to come.

I sometimes wonder how much *more* I could have benefited from the conscious practice of mindfulness during my mom's battle with cancer and my own journey of caregiving and grief—had I known what it was at the time. I could have applied it purposely for my benefit, rather than just intuitively.

Over the years, I've thought: What if my cheerleading sponsor, my fellow cheerleaders, or even Mom had patted my back on my D-Day of 1985 and said, "Don't worry. Your epic fail tryout is going to help you and your mom have the most powerful full-circle moment of your lives. Give it about twenty-one years. You'll see." I would've thought they were crazy and downright mean to say something so random and worthless to me.

If the radiologist who broke the news of Mom's cancer diagnosis on her dreadful D-Day of 2006 had signed off on the chart with a smile, looked up, and said, "Before you go, congratulations to you both on your upcoming full-circle moment that's about to take place here in this parking lot," I would've rushed Mom out the door, ready to rate Dr. Quack with a one-star review and seek a second opinion.

But now, as an adult, I get it. Thank you, God, for giving me that clarity. I sincerely believe that our heartbreaking news, our emotional pain, and our faith-based strategies were all meant to serve a bigger purpose. They showed not just me, but everyone else who reads this, that good will *always* come from the challenging times in our lives. For some, it may take a minute to realize it. For others, it may take months, years, or even an entire lifetime to see that God can make anyone's D-Days worthwhile and more powerful than they could ever imagine. The proof is right here in this book.

Chapter 2

Don't Let Them See You Sweat

"Don't slouch; put your shoulders back."
"Make sure your earrings match your outfit."
"Put some lipstick on—you look pale."
"Fix your hair—it looks like a rat's nest."

Can you tell I was the daughter of a perfectionist? And yes, this was the 1980s—hence the rat's nest hairstyle comparison. She was the kind of mom who always looked like she had it all together, despite the pressures and demands of being a wife and mother of three and later working full-time as a principal's secretary. As much as I didn't like to admit it, back then, Mom's philosophy of perfectionism made sense to me—especially when it came to coping with my epic fail of not making the varsity cheerleading squad.

As a result of the news of my demotion to the JV squad, what was supposed to be a fun and exciting spring break turned into a week of darkness. I became a zombie, vegging out on the couch for hours at a time, watching mind-numbing MTV, and consuming copious amounts of potato chips and chocolate chip ice cream. Mom did her best to cheer me up by frequently hugging me and checking on me, as well as arranging "spontaneous visits" from close friends and family.

"You doing okay?" she'd ask. "Want me to make you some chocolate chip cookies?"

As much as I was in my own pitiful world, I couldn't help but notice the look of worry on her face in response to my despair. I wanted so badly to snap out of my funk—for her sake and for mine—but I couldn't. I was stuck. Embarrassed and ashamed, I hid out in our house throughout the entire spring break.

Every once in a while, Mom would retreat into her favorite recliner and join me in watching the newly-released "We Are the World" video, which aired about every thirty minutes. Thinking she was in sync with my obsession with Lionel Richie, Michael Jackson, and the rest of the eighties icons, I'd glance over and see her emerald green rosary beads hanging off the side of the arm rest. She sure fooled me. She wasn't watching TV; she was silently praying the rosary. I'm certain my emotional well-being was at the top of her list of intentions. Shoot, if there were a Novena for cheerleaders—a specific prayer for nine days straight—Mom would've prayed that, too.

What came out of her mouth shortly after my discovery of her rosary beads had to be divinely inspired. Out of nowhere, and with a sense of renewed enthusiasm, she blurted out, "Hey, I have an idea! How about we go to the mall and get you something to wear for when you go back to school? It'll make you feel better."

What kind of fourteen-year-old would pass up an offer like that? Normally, I'd hightail it to the car, raring to go in hopes that maybe this time I'd convince her to buy me those expensive, tight, "painted-on-looking" (Mom's words) Jordache jeans I desperately wanted. But feeling like a depressed, bloated slug, the mere thought of trying on any clothes or possibly seeing my peers at the mall repulsed me.

"Nah, I don't feel like it. Not today," I groaned, staring blankly into MTV-land and covering myself in Mom's homemade afghan.

Mom counteracted my Eeyore attitude by going into full-on Tigger mode, grabbing my hand like she was about to drag me off the couch.

"Oh, come on. Let's go. It'll be fun. You never know, there might be some Jordache jeans on sale."

To my surprise, I decided to accept her proposal, realizing that her retail therapy wasn't such a bad idea. And yes, she did buy me a pair of my very own expensive, tight, painted-on-looking Jordache jeans. Of course, she also purchased light pink-tinted lip gloss and blouses to complete what was meant to be an "I'm okay" fashion statement. I was then only in a semi-funk, able to withstand longer conversations in complete sentences, backed up by a smile or two.

For my first day back at school, I wore a completely new outfit consisting of a cheery, yellow, Fiesta-style blouse, a long white flowing skirt, a bright yellow elasticized cotton belt tight at the waist, matching earrings, and ballet flats. I totally rocked the eighties look, if I say so myself.

Head held high, shoulders back, poochy stomach sucked in, and fake confidence masking my shame, I walked into class with a smile on my face. Had she been a fly on the wall, Mom would have been proud that I'd heeded her motherly advice from that morning, "No matter what people say, don't give them the satisfaction of knowing that their comments hurt. Don't let them see you sweat. You hear me?"

Her forewarnings were spot on. Though I was well-liked, I couldn't dodge the curious glances, direct questions, and even a few condolences over my demotion. It was just me and my desperate self, feeling like the scarlet letter of the school and resisting the impulse to run to the bathroom and hide. (Fortunately, there were no reenacted scenes from the movie *Mean Girls*; something tells me Mom's prayers over my return to school were the reason for that.)

Outwardly, I kept smiling. Inwardly, I plotted my return to grace. What can I say but that I learned from the best, watching Mom use her handy mantra to cope with her own challenges. Sometimes, it was almost comical to witness, like when she would be in the middle of scolding my siblings and me, and the phone would ring halfway through, interrupting her stern warnings. In a split second, she would switch into ultra-polite mode, answering the phone with a cheerful all-is-well-in-the-Lozano-household kind of hello. She nailed it every time. Of course, this was back in the days before caller ID and answering machines, so you never knew who was on the other end of the line.

But there were other times when it was harder to watch—when I almost wished Mom would've let others see her sweat a little, if only for her own relief. One example that stands out vividly in my memory is watching her navigate a challenging relationship with a difficult coworker. I like to affectionately refer to this person as Mrs. Thorn because she was a real thorn in Mom's side.

True stoic that she was, Mom held back certain details about Mrs. Thorn. But from the occasional frustrated comment that she let slip, I gathered that Mrs. Thorn was basically on the warpath to make Mom's job a living hell.

During those dreadful few years, Mom would come home from work and dump out her day's pent-up tears and frustrations. But she didn't have to say a word for me to know whether or not she'd had a bad day. All I had to do was tune in to the loud sound of her overstuffed purse slamming against the top of our washing machine as she walked through the front door. That was all I needed to tell me it was "vent time."

I'd listen as best as any young teenager could. One moment, I could sound wise and mature like Dr. Joyce Brothers: "Why don't you just tell her how you feel? She needs to know she can't treat you like that." The next moment, I'd sound like Mr. T, irrational and impulsively asking her, "Want me to go over there and beat her up?" I could tell by Mom's tears of laughter that she took to heart my candid feedback.

Unfortunately, it took a few years before deciding enough was enough. With the support from Mom's boss (the school's principal), Mrs. Thorn was confronted and reprimanded for her unprofessional ways, which led to her retirement the following year. Until that point, there was no way, no how that my mother was going to show "the thorn in her side" any vulnerability.

If you would've told me back then that Mom's masterful emotional undercover skills would one day be put to the test and change forever, I wouldn't have believed it. But it happened. I vividly remember the exact moment when she shed her old belief system, leaving me (and her as well) aware of the fact that we weren't in Kansas anymore. It occurred on the Head Shaving Day—a day when she was forced to let go.

Before I get into the details, I first have to tell you how much of a big deal having pretty hair was to Mom. You would think that lipstick was the main focus of her beauty regimen and identity, but her luscious locks came in a close second. She proudly kept up with the styles and trends of every decade of her life. You name it, she had it. The look of the early seventies featured her long, dark, silky, Cher-like style, which later morphed into the mid-length sponge-rolled look with a blast of frost color. Then, she had the salt-and-pepper colored disco afro style, not to mention the glamorous *Dynasty*-style blonde hair of the eighties. She even rocked the short blonde Annie Lennox look at one point, turning heads as people asked, "Who did your hair?"

She had every hairstyle in the book. Never did we imagine that one of those pages would be the style of a bald head.

Knowing how hard it would be to lose her hair after years of compliments from family, friends, and even strangers at the grocery store, I came up with an idea that would help ease the excruciating reality of cutting away part of her identity. Who better to assist her with the upcoming chemo-style look than those young individuals who, in Mom's eyes, hung the moon—her eight precious grandchildren?

On board and motivated to make it as fun as possible, we all met at my sister Monica's house for the official haircutting ceremony. There, my brave Mom sat at the bottom of the front porch steps so that her head could be in reach of her little barbers, ranging in age from three to thirteen. One by one, they each took turns shaving and clipping their Mimi's trademark blonde locks, which were accompanied by their sweet-sounding *whoas, oopses*, and giggles. She even let the older ones start with a little Mohawk look on her.

"Wow! Look at all that hair on the ground. You all are doing a good job cutting Mimi's hair," I told them.

Even though Mom responded in her typical upbeat Mimi fashion, praising her grandchildren for a job well done, I could tell by the slight quiver in her voice and the frozen look of her smile that seeing her hair all over the ground was painful. Still, she continued on with grace.

In the meantime, there I was, desperate Marla, pulling double duty with my periodic overprotective reactions. I kept switching back and forth, buzzing around like a Supercuts manager, whispering in Mom's ear, "You all right? Can I get you anything?"

Then, I'd switch back to mommy mode, hovering around the little ones: "Watch it with the scissors! Keep the point facing down." It seemed to me that Mom was outwardly handling it better than I was—probably because she had more years of experience not letting people see her sweat.

After all her hair was cut off, I sat on the porch steps, mesmerized by the mixture of beauty and sadness blaring from her new bald look. As Mom headed toward the dusty window to check out her new mandatory hairstyle, I immediately felt sick to my stomach. *Oh crap, Mom is going to freak out. Here it comes.*

I just knew the sensitive Mommy's girl in me had to get a grip, but it was too late. The bomb of emotions was about to detonate. With nowhere to hide, I fearfully prayed.

"Please, God; I'm scared. Give her the peace and strength to truly see herself. Please help her not to lose it."

One watery wide-eyed look and big gulp later, Mom snapped out of her trance long enough to rub her bare-skinned head. "Wow! Look at me." Each of her proud little barbers took turns hugging their Mimi, while the rest of us followed, offering her all kinds of kudos.

Of course, perfectionist that she was, there was further analysis to be had, as she calmly suggested that we go with her to the bathroom for a better look in the mirror. One look under the bright vanity lights straight into the wall-to-wall mirror was all it took for Mom's bomb to explode. There was simply no way to avoid the emotional debris headed straight toward my heart. I gave in and began to cry with her. Monica, who normally holds it together way better than Mom and I combined, held back her tears and quickly suggested, "Here, Mom, why don't you let me clean up around the edges with the buzzer. It'll look and feel even better."

Mom reluctantly agreed while visually dissecting every square inch of her head. I could definitely tell that Monica and I were on the same page, trying to distract her from another explosion.

"Oh, look, Mom," I said, directing her eyes toward the mirror. Monica stopped so Mom could see. "You have the perfect-sized head. Did you know about the huge angel kiss you've got back here?"

Right then, Mom grabbed the hand mirror to study the pinkish red, jaggedy birthmark that ran vertically from mid-center of her head down to the nape of her neck. Chuckling through her tears, she said, "Wow! I guess my hair covered it up all these years."

Now more lighthearted, all three of us agreed that Mom was ready to show off her new self and her surprise angel kiss to the rest of the family waiting outside—but not without a final touch of her pink lipstick to complete the look of her rising spirit.

She was greeted in the front yard by her adoring fans, including Dad, who happened to be undergoing his own chemo regimen at the time. Despite his shock at seeing that his wife suddenly looked like him, he threw out his notorious compliment of "You think you're hot stuff" to add his seal of approval.

When I encouraged my bald parents to take a photo together, Mom didn't reply with a pitiful, "No, I look terrible" as I would have expected of her. Surprisingly, she said, "Come on, Robert, let's do this."

Dad used to always gripe about having his picture taken, but not this time. With a calm, "okay," he gently posed next to Mom without a fuss. My guess is that he knew what a humble and monumental moment this was for her—for both of them really. The end result was a powerful image.

I choked up seeing the details of the picture up close. There was my bald, bold, and stunning mom sitting next to my bald, strong, and handsome dad. Later, I pointed out to Mom that through this picture, I realized that her beautiful hazel eyes and genuine smile would be the focal points of her attractiveness instead of her hair. She seemed so satisfied by my observation that she confidently asked, "Can I have the negative for this picture? I want to send this out to some of the family and my close friends."

What? Is this my Mom? The one who has to look perfect in front of everyone? I couldn't believe it. Prouder than I have ever been, I headed to the store the next day and had copies made for her personal fan club. When I gave them to her, I joked, "Make sure you autograph each one, okay?" I hugged her and kissed her bald head. Both of us laughed, knowing that a milestone had been reached.

It fascinated me to witness the symbolic shedding of my mother's shadow beliefs along with her hair all at the same time. Her heart was open wide enough to send out an emotional evite for others to see what a fragile yet strong, humble yet proud, and afraid yet courageous woman she had become.

It's crazy to think that it took a diagnosis of breast cancer for Mom to ban perfectionism from her mind, allowing her to not just sweat in front of everybody, but *glow*. She inspired more people than she even realized—myself included. Anytime I battle with my own perfectionism, all I have to do is look at that picture or visualize it in my mind's eye, remembering that if Mom can release her old beliefs, so can I.

Chapter 3

Be Grateful

My fragile adolescent ego couldn't take it. The thought of regressing back into my junior varsity cheerleader uniform made me want to throw up, so I decided to take the year off. Even though cheerleading had been a big part of my identity, there would be no more of it for me.

Looking back, I'm sure that decision had something to do with the melodramatic and perfectionist tendencies that I adopted as a sixteen-year-old. Going public with my perceived failure far outweighed the disappointment of sitting out on one of my all-time favorite extracurricular activities.

When I returned home from school on that dreadful Monday after spring break—a day of personal historical significance, which I have affectionately dubbed Fake-It-Till-You-Make-It Marathon Day—I immediately told Mom about my plan. While she sat there nodding her head with compassion over the whys and woes of my defeated departure, both of us unconsciously tapped into a renewed frequency, which I now realize had to be a God thing. Without hesitation, she said, "What about using this time off to get back in shape? That way, you'll be ready to make varsity by the time next year's tryouts come around."

Shocked that she had just read my mind, I giggled back, "I was just thinking that!"

With a sense of hope, we plotted my return to grace—back to the varsity squad where I belonged. All I had to do was lose twenty pounds, get in shape, perfect my techniques, and add the back handspring to my repertoire. As I write this down at my current age of forty-eight, it sounds almost impossible. But at sixteen, I wasn't wigged out by my major to-do list.

My goal was set. In a matter of minutes, I visualized myself back in my prestigious green and gold velvet varsity uniform, cheering my way through my senior year. Mom offered up her wholehearted support of my endeavor, sealing the deal with her signature hug and kiss in typical Mom fashion: "Let's do this!" she said.

For the first time in teenage daughter history, I didn't feel the need to roll my eyes or turn away from my mother's overly animated reaction. It must've had something to do with the high vibe frequency we shared in that moment. I instantly became this mature, grateful, and humble daughter—the kind my mother had been desperately praying for since the time I hit puberty.

Feeling a sense of peace, I physically and emotionally embraced her right back, understanding full well that her intentional words, "Let's do this," meant only one thing: I wouldn't have to face my challenge alone.

We didn't waste any time after that. Like two over-achievers in a pod, we began brainstorming our game plan. Both of us assumed positions in our comfy stations, with Mom rocking away in her Lazy Boy recliner and me sprawled out on the couch. I casually recited my goals, along with my self-defeating beliefs—in vivid detail.

Me: "I need to learn my back handspring. I'm such a lead foot."

Mom: "We'll have to enroll you in gymnastics."

Me: "I need to get in shape. My legs are flabby, and my stomach is poochy."

Mom: "You can use my workout videos, and we can go walking at the track."

Me: "I need to lose weight. I've gained twenty pounds. I'm too heavy to jump high, and I look frumpy."

Mom's quick and solid suggestions were, in my book, the perfect solutions. All but one, that is, which left me no choice but to regress back to my eye-rolling ways.

Mom: "Why don't you join Weight Watchers so that you can learn to eat better and lose weight the right way?"

Me: (eyes rolling) "Noooo! That's embarrassing. I don't want to. Weight Watchers is for old people."

Thankfully, my last response didn't push Mom's buttons hard enough to end the honeymoon phase of our newfound mother/daughter bond. Knowing teenagers didn't attend those kinds of meetings back then, she promised me that she'd keep it on the down low while reassuring me that Weight Watchers was still the way to go.

Never was I so humble and focused as I was that year off from cheering. While my cheerleader friends went on without me, I learned to cheer myself on from Mom's physical and emotional pats on my back. I did everything possible to buffer the sting of isolation from my previous life on the varsity squad.

At school, I buried myself in my role as Student Council Vice-President, organizing everything from the homecoming ceremony and school dances to every fundraiser under the sun. And who better to teach me the skills of leadership than my ever-so-talented former Ms. PTA mom herself? I know for a fact that she was in hog heaven, recognizing a mini version of herself in me as I bebopped my way from one activity to the next. She jokingly commented, "Look at you. Chip off the old block." (Cue the classic seventies-style gesture of blowing her knuckles and dusting off her shoulders.)

I'd laugh at her goofy antics, knowing deep down that she was right. I was like her, even if my sixteen-year-old self couldn't admit it. Shoot, as a mom myself, I now know that wasn't the only reason she was in hog heaven. She saw her daughter's content, fulfilled, determined, eye-of-the-tiger attitude during one of the most challenging times of her life. What mom wouldn't be happy about that?

By the time I got home from school every day, I still had enough energy and motivation for every sit-up and leg lift that Jane Fonda had to offer. When Mom wasn't exercising right along with me, she was in the driver's seat, hauling me to my gymnastics classes three times a week (which were almost a forty-minute drive to and from, depending on traffic). And this was all after her usual long and stressful day at work. Never once did she complain, even when I called her out on how tired she looked.

After a few weeks of witnessing Mom gracefully jump through every hoop to accomplish our original game plan, I started to get a weird feeling inside. Not in a bad way, but just different. Looking back, I understand I was on the cusp of discovering a deeper level of humility and gratitude. As much as I enjoyed her attention, I began to feel self-conscious about everything she was doing for me. The time she took to help me with school events, the money she forked over for my weekly Weight Watchers meeting and buying all those frozen meals, the cost of my gymnastics classes, and the gas for the car. It was as if God pulled up a curtain and shouted, "Ta- da! This, Marla, is what maternal sacrifice and unconditional love looks like. Stay grateful."

The concept of gratitude was nothing new to me, especially coming from a mother who was big into teaching all of her children good manners. No matter what we were doing, Mom had a way of sliding in a reminder to say *please* and *thank you* for everything in our lives. We certainly heard it the many times we headed to my grandparents' house for Christmas, prepared for our birthday parties, or went anywhere there would be a gift exchange. When my friends' parents drove me home from school or church, the first words out of Mom's mouth were, "Did you remember to thank Mr. and Mrs. so-and-so before you got out of the car?"

Every now and then, she added a teachable moment, bringing to my attention that when good things happen to you or if your prayers are answered by God, you'd better thank Him. Or if you need something, you say *please* when you pray. There I was, going through the motions of obeying Mom to the fullest, knowing early on that it was the right thing to do (plus, it made her happy). What kind of overachiever and Mommy's girl would I be to ignore that type of win/win situation?

Yet, despite knowing what it meant to say *thank you* and use good manners, I had seldom truly felt the emotion that was supposed to go along with it. Most of the time, I was just reciting the words that Mom had taught me. Up until that moment of realization at age sixteen, when it finally hit me how much time, money, and effort Mom was giving to help me succeed, I didn't understand what it meant to be genuinely grateful.

The kinder, gentler teenage version of me started to throw out random *pleases* and *thank yous*—without even being told—toward my mom, who was my life coach, financial supporter, chauffeur, and prayer warrior all rolled into one. She was even shocked by my transformation. Often, she randomly smiled and thanked me for thanking her.

I'm proud to say that during our game plan year (with only a few minor glitches here and there), not only did I succeed in maintaining my newly discovered outlook, but Mom and I managed to stay on that same high frequency we'd found. Neither of us had any idea that this frequency would one day come in handy during the later season of our lives when she was battling cancer.

❧

Unfortunately, it didn't take long—a week, to be exact—for the bald look, the picture-taking, the wig, and all the rest of the hoopla from Mom's hair shaving day to run its course.

"What's the matter?" I asked when I walked in her house, toting my bubbly four-year-old twin boys.

Mom looked pale and deflated as she desperately tried to greet us in her traditional "peppy Mimi" way. Even the bright red bandana around her head and the perfectly matched lipstick couldn't mask the despair radiating from her body. I knew right then that our after-noon plans of shopping and eating out would be either delayed or cancelled. While the twins darted back and forth between Mimi and their toys, she lay on the couch, venting about how weak she felt, how frustrated she was about not feeling like herself, how bad she looked bald, and how scared she felt about her prognosis. Right away, my heart sank, reminding me that I still hadn't outgrown my Mommy's girl tendency of absorbing every ounce of her physical and emotional pain.

Everything out of her mouth was so negative that I thought I would never see my spunky, healthy, faith-filled Mom ever again. *Damn you, cancer. Look what you're do-ing to her. Please, God, help me help Mom. I can't stand seeing her this way. Take this away from her. Please.*

I had, of course, hoped that she would somehow by-pass the side effects of chemo. But who was I trying to fool? I was a nurse, for crying out loud. I knew better. I knew from witnessing my patients, my own dad, and other cancer-stricken family members and friends just how insidious the dark side of treatment can be.

God was kind enough to answer my frantic plea rather quickly, defusing my defensive, over-my-dead-body-am-I-going-to-let-Mom-get-to-that-dark-side attitude so that I could get to the place where He wanted me to go.

I patiently listened to her litany of woes and her brave confession of feeling so depressed that all she wanted to do was lie down on the couch and watch endless hours of HGTV and Project Runway. It was then that I suddenly recognized something powerful. *Look at this. Same living room, same couch, same TV, same depressive funk from my teenage days—except this time, the tables have turned. Oh, my God. Mom is me, and I'm Mom.*

It felt like a scene from Freaky Friday, minus the comedy. While my mother's situation was certainly more serious than mine had been when I was fourteen, I felt like I was seeing her play the Marla role in a reenactment scene from spring break 1985. That realization led me to do the only thing that made sense—follow her example.

Mimicking her maternal support, I sprang into action, busying myself during her initial week in a funk by supplying her stash of favorite junk food and Rocky Road ice cream, taking her out to buy cool outfits and head accessories for chemo days, and distracting her with invitations to sleepovers and the grandkids' school activities. When her fatigue called the shots over my well-intentioned, action-packed agenda, I spent time on the couch with her oohing, ahhing, and critiquing house renovations and fashion trends on TV. She was slowly coming around again.

Every ounce of Mommy's girl in me was in awe. It wasn't just seeing Mom back to her positive, upbeat self, but also the fact that another full-circle moment had made its way into our lives.

Unfortunately, the old saying, "What goes up must come down," started to become my secret motto during Mom's bleaker days. It was becoming obvious to me that our go-to strategies from our once-successful mother/ daughter boot camps were no longer so effective in the face of cancer. The cumulative effects of her treatments were making it harder for her to rebound from her unwanted side effect of negativity.

What am I supposed to do now, Lord? I hate seeing her this way. Show me how to help her through this damn cancer.

To my surprise, God instantly unveiled an old vision from that monumental humility moment when I was sixteen. Except this time, when He raised the curtain, all I saw were HIS words: "Stay Grateful."

Tuned into the Holy Spirit, I sobbed over such simple, loving instructions. Like a movie trailer, God kept featuring all the "Mom and Me" thank-you scenes from years past. Her spiel before gift exchanges. Her questioning my expression of verbal appreciation to the people who drove me home. Her reminders for me to pray my thanks. Her nudges to write thank-you notes to family, friends, teachers, and wedding guests.

But it was the last scene, the one from the 1990s, involving me, Mom, and Oprah Winfrey, that God used to show me the how-to behind his "Stay Grateful" message. I flashed back to the time when I was a new mother myself, and Mom was a new Mimi. We were in front of the TV watching my favorite queen of talk show hosts. Four o'clock on weekdays was the golden hour in my book—an hour where I learned the meaning of loving myself, gratitude, and self-care (and, of course, Oprah's favorite things).

The next day, trying to contain my enthusiasm as we waited in the crowded oncology office, I casually reintroduced the sweet memory of our gratitude season. "Hey, Mom, remember how we used to watch Oprah at my house when Natalie was a baby?"

With a reflective look on her face, she smiled. "Of course, I do."

"Remember how we liked the episodes when Oprah talked about gratitude, especially that one guest who promoted her gratitude journal?"

Before I could finish my sentence, Mom interrupted, "Yeah, you bought both of us a copy of her gratitude journal from Barnes & Noble. Every night, we wrote down five things we were grateful for. That journal helped me through a lot of things. Especially the time when Popo got sick and after he died." (Popo was Mom's beloved father—my grandfather.)

Without pause, I executed God's new game plan for us. "How about we do that again? Just like the good ol' days. Let's get ourselves another journal so that we can keep track of all the things we're grateful for while you go through chemo. I know it'll help you get through all this."

Totally on board, Mom accepted my offer and suggested we stop by Walgreens to pick up a few small spiral notebooks—her treat.

Riding on the day's high-vibe frequency, I eagerly called Mom that night to remind her to jot down her thank-yous before she went to bed. Upbeat and to the point, she replied, "I did already. I wrote that I was thankful for God's help getting me through this day, that my CT scan was all clear, for my family and friends, for the sweet cards I got in the mail, and for this gratitude journal idea."

I can't describe the feeling of relief that came over me when I heard my mom sound like her old positive self. In my head, I kept repeating: *Thank you, God.* I knew this new game plan was Mom's perfect remedy.

From that point on, we entertained each other back and forth as we verbally exchanged the details of our sometimes giddy, often serious thankful entries. Over the next few weeks, It was obvious that Mom's mood and outlook were on the upswing—so much so that in an attempt to beat her chemo brain to the punch, she decided to carry her handy dandy notebook in her purse, ready to jot down any of her spontaneous moments of gratitude.

Sure, Mom still had her low days mixed with crappy side effects and emotional funk, but not nearly to the degree she'd experienced previously. She rebounded quicker and became more focused, ready to beat cancer the good old-fashioned Mom way, with faith, gratitude, and strength.

As I think back on this time, I wonder if Mom ever connected the dots from our successful game plan of 2006 back to the successful game plan of 1985 in the same way I'm doing now. If she did, she must have quietly tucked it away in her heart. Either way, I know that as I write this, Mom and I are on the same familiar frequency, if not a higher one now, praising God for all of His creative ways in showing us just how powerful gratitude can be in our everlasting mother/daughter bond.

Chapter 4

Thanks Be to God and All That Good Stuff

I sat on the cafeteria floor of my elementary school with my friends, watching my mother pound her little wooden gavel as she stood behind the podium. Every time, she'd start the meeting with her standard judge-like introduction: "This meeting is now called to order." Every time, I internally giggled, thinking how silly it all sounded. Especially the part when she motioned for a vote: "All in favor, say 'aye.' All opposed?" My friends and I would chime in with a loud and goofy "aye," having no clue what our unsolicited vote even meant. We just wanted Mom and the rest of the PTA officers to hurry it up and end the meeting so that we could get to the cookies and punch table in the back of the cafeteria.

Mom was a model PTA president—not just at my elementary and middle schools, but also at the district level. It was this time in the seventies and eighties when her gift of leadership came to light.

It was obvious to me that she was a natural in her esteemed position. The proof was in the kudos from other PTA officers, faculty, staff, and parents who stayed after the meetings to voice their appreciation for her graceful, likable, and organized style. By then, there was no need to hurry things up. More kudos meant seconds and thirds in the refreshment line, which was fine with me.

Mom used to jokingly claim that her position as President of the Elvis Fan Club in 1955 was her first leadership role. If you watched how effortlessly she interacted with people, you'd never guess that shyness was part of her childhood history. Friendly, talkative, and always "others oriented," she could connect with anybody, no matter who they were—bank teller, cashier at the grocery store, fellow church or PTA member, friend, relative, or even a total stranger. Of course, I always regretted that strong point every time she stopped and talked to random people in the frozen food section of the grocery store. I can recall countless instances of standing by the grocery cart madder than a hornet during those long-winded conversations she called "chats." *Dang it, why does it always have to happen here? She's taking forever. Can't she see I'm shivering and about to get frostbite? Let's go, Mom, hurry up.*

My self-centered thoughts faded once Mom tuned in to poor little ol' me. All it took was a few of my go-to tactics, which consisted of clearing my throat numerous times in my uniquely audible fashion while I passive-aggressively maneuvered the grocery basket. She got the hint and graciously said her goodbyes as we headed toward the nearby bread aisle, where I finally had the chance to thaw out.

During Mom's tenure as school district president, she worked alongside a sweet woman—for the sake of this story, let's call her Mrs. Jones. In my eyes, Mrs. Jones appeared way older than my mother. She had big blue eyes, sported fresh-from-the-beauty-parlor bouffant hair, and wore brightly-colored lipstick that outlined her big smile. She used her loud and jovial voice at record speed. In short, she was quite the talker.

One hot summer day, when Dad was out of town, Mom decided to treat our family to our favorite weekly fix at Wendy's. Mom's standard homemade dish of meat, vermicelli, and beans two to three times a week wreaked havoc with both our taste buds and her nerves. Let's just say that when it came to cooking, Mom was no Julia Child—EXCEPT when it came to baking her famous chocolate chip cookies (that's a different story).

So when Mom offered to pick up our favorite hamburger combos via drive-thru, I jumped right in with a counteroffer: "If I go with you, can you get me a frosty?"

Mom made no qualms about my deal, knowing she would add to that order with a chocolate frosty of her own. "Okay, but on the way there, I've gotta stop by Mrs.

Jones's house to give her these papers." My sweet tooth reminded me to hold back my sour attitude over the detour announcement.

"Hi, Sandra! Come on in!" Mrs. Jones shouted as she opened her front screen door.

Halfway up her sidewalk, Mom couldn't help but increase her pace to match the intensity of Mrs. Jones's bold greeting. Mom turned her head and mouthed to me, "I'll be right back," trying to reassure me that *this* time, the visit wouldn't be long. *Yeah right,* I thought sarcastically. *Not when you're with Mrs. Jones.*

What was supposed to be minutes felt like hours of waiting. Maybe it was the early onset of a heat stroke that made the ticking sound of my Timex watch seem as if it was hooked up to THX surround sound. It felt like a scene from a movie. Each tick and tock seemed synchronized to each bead of sweat that fell from my face.

As I waited in the car with the windows rolled down (yes, it was safe to do that back then), I contemplated getting out to relieve my gross sweaty legs from the wrath of the sweltering car seat. Panicky and possibly delusional from the heat (with a dash of post-traumatic stress), I had to keep reminding myself that the car seat was made of fabric and not like the vinyl seats from our previous station wagon. Therefore, I wasn't going to get third degree burns on the back of my delicate thighs.

Torn between standing outside of the car, within view of a bunch of boys playing football in the street or melting in the car for "just a few more minutes," I chose the latter. (Some of those boys were former rowdy classmates of mine and frequent flyers at the principal's office.) I was already annoyed and didn't need any more stress to raise my body temperature, so I decided to stay put and simmer. It was at that moment I realized that being stuck in the dairy aisle hadn't been so bad after all. *Mom, hurry up already!*

It seemed the trend back then was always trying to hurry up Mom. She must have received my complaints telepathically because just when I thought I couldn't take it anymore, out she walked with PTA folders in hand, cordially smiling and nodding at Mrs. Jones's nonstop monologue on the way to the car. Every other line I heard from Mrs. Jones's enthusiastic tone was: "Thank you, Jesus. Praise God, and thanks be to God."

I found myself shocked and confused—and painfully aware of her run-on sentences. *How can someone say all those nice things about God in the same breath and not even be at church?* I wondered. In my world, those types of phrases only appeared in songs or readings during a Catechism class or Sunday mass.

I could tell that Mrs. Jones's outward expression of her Christian faith also made my conservative Catholic mom uncomfortable. At that time, Mom kept her praises undercover, and words of faith were strictly reserved for her immediate family and closest friends. That was all she knew. Except for the spring of 1977, that is, when our neighbor, Gary Jacobs, passed away unexpectedly at age fifteen from Reye's Syndrome, a deadly reaction to aspirin that can occur when treating a virus. It was the kind of tragedy that was nearly impossible for my immediate family and the rest of our neighborhood community to wrap our brains around. How could this healthy, happy, cute, freckled-faced redhead who used to play basketball in our backyard and listen to 8-track tapes with my older brother suddenly be gone?

Even though I was only eight years old when he died, I remember the somberness that lingered in our home for weeks following his death and how scared I was to go in our backyard. I was afraid of seeing his bereaved parents and little sister crying in their yard. It was as if grief was going to jump the fence, cross the alley, and walk right through our back gate the same way Gary used to.

As a mom myself today, I now understand the kind of impact such incidents have on a mother's heart, and I can relate to my own mother's spiritual shift. She became a kind of Prayer Warrior. It was rare for me to see her in action in that way. A few times, I overheard her tell Mrs. Jacobs that we would pray for them, and Mom kept her promise. She rallied her little troop to pray the Rosary for Gary and his bereaved family.

Honestly, at that age, I didn't particularly enjoy praying the Rosary. It was normal for me to cringe and fidget my way through the twenty minutes of kneeling next to

Mom's bed, hyper-focused on making sure my finger was on the right bead while trying to stay in unison with her flow of Our Fathers and Hail Marys. But there was something different this time around. I was in rare form, participating with stillness, grace, and a whole lot of mindfulness. Maybe it had to do with the special intention behind our nightly ritual. Maybe Mom's warrior-like spirit was contagious. Or maybe it had to do with my being in tune with her quivering voice every time she recited the words: "And may perpetual light shine upon him." Whatever the case, I witnessed Mom channel her faith at a whole other level—but still not anywhere near the level of Mrs. Jones.

Peeking her head through the window as Mom started the car, Mrs. Jones joyfully blurted out, "God bless you two! Goodbye!"

"You too," Mom replied awkwardly.

As we drove off, I wasted no time in asking, "Is she Catholic?"

"No, she's a Protestant," Mom quickly answered, turning the A/C on full blast.

"What's that mean?"

Right then and there, Mom's big ol' honkin', green 1977 Ford LTD transformed into a classroom for the crash course of Different Faiths 101. I learned that not everybody is a Catholic, and sometimes, people (like Mom) can feel uncomfortable with the unfamiliarity of how those of different faiths express their love for God. That was my mom's strong opinion—until cancer came along.

Midway through her journey with cancer, I started to notice an eye-opening trend. Every time Mom revealed good news of scan reports and medical updates, whether verbally, via email, or through a handwritten note, she always signed off with either "Thanks be to God," "Praise God," "Thank you, Jesus," or "God Bless You." And she always made generous use of exclamation marks—either written or implied in her speech—as a way of emphasizing her genuine love and gratitude toward God. Mom's new mantra was to give credit where credit was due, not only for herself but for others like me, who would learn from her.

And she lived by that mantra, even when things didn't go as planned. Through every setback, whether an unexpected chemo side effect of thrush or plantar fasciitis, an appointment that ran longer than it was supposed to, or an extended wait time on lab results, Mom continued to find the blessings to balance them out—always keeping God front and center.

Like most normal human beings, Mom had her fair share of not-so-good days when her mantra didn't work. Desperado that I was, I'd gather my spiritual ammunition and hunt down that very motto along with her other catchphrases, favorite Bible verses, and even a few Rocky Balboa pep talks to help battle the doubts, fears, and physical pain that she was enduring.

Thankfully, her resilience allowed her to rebound quickly. Oh, what a happy Mommy's girl I was whenever I saw her get back in the game. It seemed that with each rebound came another spiritual shift. In fact, I couldn't keep up with her changes. I started to notice her transformation much like I did back in 1977. I'd often ask myself, *Who is this woman? Where is my conservative Catholic Mom from back in the day? Does she even realize how she sounds? How she acts?* Not that what I was seeing was a bad thing—heavens no! It was inspiring to witness her spiritual growth before my eyes, and it was impossible to ignore. One day, however, I couldn't help myself. I called her out on it.

It happened right after a chemo appointment. On our way out, Mom made a beeline toward her favorite nurse, Suzanne, to hug her goodbye. She boldly exclaimed to Suzanne, "See you next week. God bless you!"

We left arm-in-arm, relieved that another chemo treatment was behind us. "Okay, Mrs. Jones, let's go," I smirked.

Mom smirked back like she knew exactly what I meant, but she probed nonetheless. "What?" she asked innocently.

59

"Remember back in the day, when you couldn't understand Mrs. Jones's outward expression of faith and love for God? And now here you are doing it yourself."

Affirming my trip down memory lane, Mom explained, "Yeah, I know. When you go through this kind of stuff, all that is out the window. You don't care what others think. You just say how you feel."

We both agreed that our ideas and opinions had changed in response to spiritual shifts in our lives, validating Mrs. Jones's special reflection of God's grace that was powerful enough for others to see and feel. That simple acknowledgement was Mom's way of updating her 1977 crash course of "Different Faiths 101," teaching me that openly sharing our faith in God, whether through words or actions, can lead us toward hope and love.

Chapter 5

We Did It

"Marla, Get ready, you're up next."

There's nothing like a dose of reality to snap you out of a heavenly trance of Hail Marys. That was me. The moment had arrived. Spring cheerleading tryouts, 1986. Standing there, while waiting my turn in the stinky girls' locker room, my nerves were on overdrive. No matter how hard I tried, I couldn't stop the excitement, fear, and sheer determination from infusing through every cell of my body. I also couldn't help the fact that my infusion had a nagging ingredient of some post-traumatic nerves from my last epic fail tryout.

Oh my God, what if I mess up? What if I don't make it again?

Panic-stricken, I quickly reminded myself of the achievements that had gotten me there in the first place. *Look, you're twenty pounds lighter and in the best shape you've ever been. You know how to do the back handspring, plus your jumps are even higher than before. Stop worrying and remember: God is going to help you.*

Hanging on to each word of my internal pep talk, a sense of peace came over me, allowing me to forget about my self-doubt and the stench of sweaty tennis shoes emanating from the lockers.

Leaning over to my friend who was next in line—and whose nerves were just as fragile as mine—I desperately asked, "Quick! Look! Do I still have my lipstick on?"

Sweet Kelly. My one and only cheerleader friend going all the way back to the sixth grade, who never once abandoned me during my year on the sidelines. There she was again, supporting me through yet another season with her kind and dutiful lipstick inspection. Smiling through her nerves, she replied, "Yes, it's still on. You're going to do great. Good luck!"

I stood there, all decked out in my crisp, custom-made, one-piece, yellow and white bloomer outfit, wondering: *What just happened to our gym?* The once small and familiar athletics room had somehow morphed into a massive arena before my eyes. Everything around me was a bigger version of itself on steroids. The tryout monitors looked like club bouncers guarding the door. If I didn't know any better, I would've thought the three judges sitting across the gym were about to crucify me. Even the dull silence and the low lighting of the gym felt like a scene from a horror movie. Closing my eyes, I took a deep breath and prayed, *Please, God, be with me now.* I opened my eyes and felt pure relief as everything around me deflated back to normal.

Cramming in one last hurried and heartfelt Hail Mary, I tumbled my way into the gym, showing everyone—including myself—the power of true grit, God's grace, and a mother/daughter synchronized prayer. (Mom later told me that she was holding her own private prayer vigil at our local parish during the time of my performance.)

Floating on a cloud of adrenaline, I felt bionic, like an all-American cheerleader whose voice was louder than ten megaphones and who could jump and kick high enough to reach the gym ceiling.

"Ready? Okay!" I shouted. I don't remember much after that except the sweet wink and nod from one of the judges in response to my back handspring as I walked off the gym floor. I wanted so badly to yell out to her: *Do you know anything about me? Do you know how far I've come? Please, pick me! Pick me!*

In true fake-it-till-you-make-it form, I graciously exited stage left directly into the crowded gym classroom to join my fellow wigged-out hostages—I mean cheerleader candidates. We stuffed our faces with junk food and melodramatic critiques of our own respective routines. I couldn't stop the one-sided dialogue in my head, begging God to grant me a good score as I repeated countless Hail Marys in between prayers.

What felt like eternity was actually only three hours later. Results were finally in. I burst through the prison gate where dreams come true and ran across the parking lot to where my parents and sister were anxiously waiting. Jumping, arms raised in victory, I hollered, "I made it! I made it!"

While Dad and Monica (the non-criers in the family) valiantly choked back tears, Mom wept freely and joyfully. Our exchange felt like a scene from Rocky when he hugs his trainer, Mickey, after winning the big fight. (Like many memories from my past, this one from my victorious day gets me every time. I'm even crying as I write this.)

Mom kept repeating in my ear: "I'm so proud of you, honey," as she hugged and kissed me. Overwhelmed with emotion, I happily accepted her praise, knowing in my heart that this was her victory, too.

I wish I could say the intensity of the magical moment lasted the rest of the evening, but it didn't. Upon arriving home, I headed straight to my lifeline—the one with the long cord that hung near the kitchen sink—to share the good news with my best friend since kindergarten. Before I lifted the receiver, Mom admonished me sternly: "Listen, young lady, before you get on that phone, you'd better get in your room, kneel down, and thank God for answering our prayers."

Talk about a killjoy. I rolled my eyes. "I will, Mom. Just let me call Sabrina first."

"No ma'am," she insisted through gritted teeth, her finger pointed toward my bedroom. "Get in there now!"

Stomping toward my room, I again rolled my eyes in protest, trying to ignore my mother as she muttered,

"Oh, how easy one forgets." Instantly, I became annoyed—annoyed with myself for not having made thanking God my priority and annoyed with Mom for telling me what to do.

Looking back, I should've known better. I blame the combination of my own immaturity and the distracting fanfare of the day as the culprits of my spiritual mishap.

In my room, surrounded by my bright yellow walls covered in Lionel Richie posters, I knelt down next to my bed and prayed, "Dear God, thank you for letting me make the varsity team." Engulfed in a sense of peace, I tearfully continued, "Thank you for answering my prayers and for being with me. I love you."

As I opened my bedroom door and made a dash back to the kitchen, my well-intended watchdog hugged me and said, "*Now* you can go use the phone!"

Embraced in Mom's arms, my gratitude for God solidified. I wonder if she felt that through my lingering hug. Did she know that her teachings were finally worming their way into my head, heart, and soul? Maybe she could tell by the sincerity in my voice, the tightness in my hug, and my watery eyes as I confessed, "I could not have done this without God *and* you. Thank you, Momma. You helped me so much."

We boo-hooed a bit and exchanged more kisses, you're-welcomes, and I-love-yous before Mom playfully slapped my butt. "Now, go make your phone call, miss varsity cheerleader."

"Hi, Mrs. Lozano. You ready?"

Who knew that twenty years later, a simple dose of reality could have the same effect as my cheerleader tryouts so long ago, inducing another heavenly trance of Hail Marys. Yep, that's how I rolled, still relying on my faith in God and my silent rosary prayer that always played in my head in the midst of life's most gut-wrenching moments.

This appointment was a big deal. We were supposed to talk to Mom's oncologist before her regularly scheduled chemo treatment to find out the results of her most recent CT scan. I was scared out of my wits. Outwardly, I appeared calm and bright, gliding my way around Mom, traffic, and office space, while inwardly, I was doing my best to tame the anxious, fearful beast that reared its ugly head in the back of my mind. Incessant thoughts of, *What if this chemo isn't working?* morphed into a haphazard dialogue with God and His ever most patient Mother Mary.

Despite her usual brave front, Mom let her guard down right there in in the packed waiting room. "God, I hope these results come back clear. I'm so scared." Holding back tears, she added, "I just have to keep on praying and trusting that God is going to heal me, no matter what, right?"

Doing what I do best, I absorbed every ounce of Mom's emotional pain. Suddenly, I was carrying on two conversations, one with Mom and one with God. Holding Mom's hand, I replied, "You're right, Mom. We have to keep praying and trusting," while simultaneously praying silently: *Please God, bless Momma. Give her peace and strength, and let these scans be clear.*

Looking back, I am one hundred percent sure it was God and His creative ways that came to the rescue to help release Mom and me from the chains of our bipolar frenzy between faith and fear.

Just moments after our heartfelt exchange, our eyes were drawn to the TV as a rowdy contestant on *The Price is Right* was jumping up and down like a madman, celebrating his victory in the Showcase Showdown. Before either of us had a chance to comment on it, a frail, pale, older woman sweetly approached Mom.

"Excuse me," she whispered. "Every time I see you in this waiting room, you always look so good. What's your secret?"

Totally caught off guard, I glanced at Mom, who didn't miss a beat in answering this woman's question—almost as if the whole scene was somehow rehearsed. Popping her purse open, Mom eagerly rummaged around before holding up her prized possession, glimmering in its shiny gold tube. On cue, she kindly looked back at the sweet woman with her dark recessed eyes and ashen skin, proudly declaring, "Faith and a Tube of Lipstick!"

The fact that Mom had immediately located her lipstick among the many contents of her overstuffed purse was a feat in itself. I exchanged polite smiles with our unexpected guest. What I really felt like doing was giving her a big hug for serving as God's ambassador that day, helping us to come out of our worried funk. But I didn't have time; just seconds after our brief conversation, we heard the nurse's voice call out: "Mrs. Lozano, you ready?"

Both of us shot up and quickly gathered our things before proceeding to the exam room. "God bless you," Mom said to the woman, walking away with a friendly wave. My heart was beating a mile a minute in anticipation of the results we were about to receive. Putting on a brave face and cramming in one last Hail Mary, I raced to keep up with Mom's hurried pace as she marched toward the nurse.

Right before the oncologist came into the exam room, we were surprised by Dad's impromptu visit from work so that he could be there as the final verdict was delivered. His surprise arrival was yet another distraction brought to us by God to free us from our unwelcome thoughts of worry. We greeted Dad and brought him up to speed on the events of the day. "I'll be able to tell if it's good or bad news based on how quickly Dr. Tolcher enters the room and how big his smile is," Mom predicted.

And just like that, our worlds changed as the man himself entered the exam room with a huge smile on his face, revealing right away that the chemo was indeed working. "Scans all clear," he proclaimed as he proudly handed us the radiology report. The words "no evidence of cancer" jumped off the page and straight into our hearts.

Always sensitive to the fragile emotions of the patients on the other side of the less-than-soundproof walls of the doctor's office, we contained our exhilaration with quiet tears of joy, hugs, and Mom's simple rejoicing prayer: "Thank you, God. Thank you." Fortunately, Mom's oncologist, Dr. Tolcher, was the type of doctor who welcomed our expressions of faith, as well as Mom's spontaneous hugs and kisses.

We practically floated out of the office. I was on such a high that I had to stop myself from doing cartwheels down the hallway and shouting, "*Woo-hoo! Thank you, Jesus! All clear! You hear that, everyone? Mom's all clear!*"

But instead, we waited until we got into the parking lot to spaz out. (It seemed we often had our gut-wrenching or soul-shifting experiences in parking lots.) We fell into a reenactment scene from my tryout victory of 1986—with the added twist of a meaningful role reversal. While Dad choked back his tears, Mom and I went round and round, embracing and kissing each other. Somehow, I was able to interrupt her unceasing praises to God. "I'm so proud of you, Mom. Just a few more treatments to go, and you're done."

"Thank you, honey," she nodded. "I feel so blessed."

I felt the same way—and by the look on Dad's face, I could tell he did, too.

Even though Mom had the good news to sustain her hope through the following treatments, we still kept up our gratitude game plan to ward off any lingering effects of fatigue, nausea, and general blah-ness from her stringent chemo regimen.

A few weeks after the "all clear" appointment, Mom and I were sitting in the waiting room for one of her treatments. She was just a few appointments shy of her final treatment when I noticed something. I spotted the same lady from before who had asked Mom about her secret for looking good. But this time, she was sitting noticeably taller and prouder, and her complexion boasted a radiant glow. As our eyes locked, she smiled, almost as if she noticed how impressed I was with the change in her demeanor.

I enthusiastically patted Mom's leg and blurted out, "Mom, look!"

"What?" Mom responded in her stop-smacking-my-knee voice.

Almost dancing in my chair, I exclaimed, "That's the lady who came up to you and asked about your secret. Look how good she looks!"

When Mom glanced her way, the sweet lady reached into her purse, pulled out a tube of lipstick and proudly waved it in the air. It was obvious that she wanted us to know she had taken Mom's advice.

Being so tuned into the moment, I felt as if that lady was again a fill-in for God, holding up a gigantic mirror to show us His reflection of love, mercy, and goodness. I wanted so badly for Mom to see what I saw, to feel what I felt.

"Gosh, Mom. You don't even know this lady, and you touched her life like that," I said with a dramatic snap of my fingers.

Mom tried to shrug off my compliment. "I did?"

In the back of my mind, I knew she knew better. She was the one who taught me to see things in that way, yet she dismissed it when the shoe was on the other foot. Blame it on her track record of reluctance to accept compliments—or maybe her chemo brain was doing the talking that day. Whatever the reason, I had to put the mirror in her face.

"Yeah, you did!" I assured her.

She looked at me and grinned. "Yeah, I guess so."

I hugged her, hoping that all the gratitude energy that had just welled up in my heart would seep straight into hers. And it did.

"I'm just so thankful," she said, closing her eyes in relief. "So thankful."

If my current reflective self could've appeared to my stressed out thirty-something self in that parking lot and that waiting room back in 2006, I would have asked, *"Do you see it, Marla? Do you see the correlation between your victories and your mom's? Wasn't that amazing, the way you mirrored back Mom's teachings of faith, hard work, and gratitude whenever she became vulnerable, just like you were back in the day? Crazy, right?"*

Part of me thinks I would have answered in the same way Mom responded to me. *"Ummm ... yeah, I guess so."*

Of course, back then, I couldn't see the impact of the moment clearly like I can now. I was in too much pain and stress and too involved in the busyness of fulfilling my overachieving, sandwich-generation role to see the spiritual aha moment that was before me. Only in *His* perfect timing would God reveal how significant those episodes would be in my life. Now, I can say with confidence and conviction, "I'm just so thankful. So thankful."

With God's perfect game plan, we did it—all three of us.

Chapter 6

Sweet Victory

*Y*ay me! For as long as I can remember, early mornings were never a prime time for me to feel or much less express any kind of excitement—except for the times in early childhood when Saturday cartoons ruled my life. But this particular morning was different. It was the morning of my first high school football game as a new senior varsity cheerleader. After the second round of pressing the snooze button to my annoying alarm, which I believe was the culprit to my many cranky spanky morning moods, I was awakened by the familiar sound of Mom's house shoes brushing up against the carpet, along with a strange tinkling sound. I thought I was dreaming until I felt her kiss me on the cheek and heard her loving and very personalized wake-up call: "Time for all varsity cheerleaders to wake up and get ready for their first morning pep rally and football game. Wake up, Tinky."

I had forgotten the sweetness behind Mom's unique strategy of luring me out of bed during those wee hours of the morning when I lay comatose snuggled under the covers. It had been a long time, probably middle school, since I'd last heard one of her wake-up fun forecasts. Feeling energized by my impromptu personal alarm, I opened my eyes to find Mom standing there proudly, holding something that I had been without for over a year: my very own green and gold football mum with mini cowbells and charms dangling from it.

If you're a non-Texan wondering what exactly a football mum is, let me explain. In Texas, one of the many highlights during the fall semester in high school was wearing a homecoming football mum. Imagine an enormous corsage. Each consisted of a pale yellow or white chrysanthemum—a real one, not a fake one. Hanging from the corsage's cardboard base were oodles of school-colored ribbons that were long and wide enough to be decorated with glittery words, cute charms, and shiny mini cowbells. It used to be given by boyfriends during the day of a homecoming game, but by the mid to late eighties, it was not only acceptable to receive the highly coveted mum from friends but even parents. I also loved the fact that it was no longer restricted to the day of a homecoming game. We could prance around the hallways to show off our school pride whenever we wanted—a new tradition that my older sister, Monica, didn't like. Often, she'd question Mom with the "why does Marla get a mum every week when all I got was one during homecoming?" I couldn't help the fact that volleyball players didn't receive the same mum recognition as cheerleaders. I mean, what was Mom supposed to do? She had to keep up with the Joneses, following the other cheer moms' weekly traditions. Since mums were meant to be seen, we cheerleaders made sure that showcasing our mums didn't end just because the school day was over. Oh no, not us. Before each football game started, we had to proudly display our enormous green and gold accessories from the mouthpieces of our megaphones.

I loved having a mum—so much that sometimes, I'd ignore the fact it could weigh down the right shoulder of my uniform, leave me lopsided, and cause the safety pin to wear a hole in the fabric. I didn't care if it left a trail of glitter or mum petals on my uniform, school desk, or even the seat of my car. I didn't even care how goofy I looked (well, maybe a little) every time I had to chase it down from the fall winds that knocked it off my megaphone.

Having been a mum connoisseur since the seventh grade, each one that was given to me—whether from my parents, a boy I was dating, or a sweet friend—made me feel special. But it was the one from Mom that immediately became my all-time favorite—the one with the mini cowbell clanking that woke me from my half-comatose state that early morning.

As I sat up in bed, I couldn't help but home in on the glittered words blaring from one of the shiny green ribbons. Smack dab in the middle of the standard ribbons that held the common words, "Go Cowboys" and "Class of '87" was the phrase, "YOU DID IT." Totally in sync, I wiped the sleep from my eyes, Mom wiped her tears, and she added one last spin to her creative wake-up call:

"Time for girls like you to wake up so that they can wear their comeback mums on their big day. Here you go. Wear it with pride, you hear me?"

"Yes, I will. Thank you, Momma."

To this day, I still wonder if Mom requested that the florist strategically position that "YOU DID IT" ribbon so that all would see it. Maybe she did; maybe she didn't. All I know is that I was glad it was in full view for my classmates and teachers to notice it.

I had questions coming at me left and right, asking what those three little words meant. I didn't care about sounding like a broken record. I proudly shared the meaning with anyone who would listen, offering both long and short versions of the story and giving credit where credit was due.

In between my public announcements, I thought, *What a difference a year makes. Look at me! I'm not having to fake it till I make it anymore. This is real. I made it. Thank you, God.* I had returned to a state of grace. I had grown up before my very own eyes, realizing that the sweet details stemming from the heartbreak of my epic fail tryouts had all been true gifts.

When my high school glory days were over, it was hard to let go. So I decided to keep all of my mums, hanging them on my wall at my parents' house until my second year of college. Even as the flower petals became sparse, and the glittered ribbons faded with age, my eyes were always drawn to my comeback ribbon, reminding me of my inner strength given to me by God. Little did I know that Mom's divinely inspired idea would one day resurface when it was her time to shine.

⁂

The countdown was almost over. We were down to the final hours of what would be Mom's last chemo day.

"Let's get this show on the road," she'd say. Lord knows how many times I heard her common catchphrase when it was time to get something done or get out of the house. And here she was saying it to her nurse, Christine. I wanted to laugh, but I couldn't. Mom didn't know that I was standing behind her. I wanted to make her feel special during that momentous occasion just like she had always done for me throughout the highlights and heartbreaks of my life.

Hoping Christine wouldn't blow my cover, I secretly winked at her. Then, I tiptoed around Mom as she sat in her treatment chair. It was obviously a big day for her and for all of us who loved her. And with that big day came big surprises. I tried my best to keep my full throttle mind in order, coordinating not just my undercover gift, but the behind-the-scenes visit from her two sisters (breast cancer survivors themselves) and niece for post-treatment balloon release and lunch at Cracker Barrel.

Inhaling a deep breath of thanks, I gently approached Mom and exhaled love.

"Time for last-time chemo patients to get the show on the road!" I said, my voice quivering.

Shocked by my sneakiness and the floral arrangement with pink ribbon sash that dangled in her face, Mom replied, "Oh! Hi, honey." Tears welled up in her eyes. "What's this?"

"Gotta commemorate your big day," I said, handing over her flowers.

"Oh, honey, thank you."

More and more, I could feel the dam swelling. I'm pretty sure Christine was feeling it, too. She must have been a Mommy's girl herself or just one of those gifted intuitive nurses because she quickly moved the IV pole out of the way, making room for my big reveal and the emotional hug that was to follow.

I could hardly contain my joy as I watched Mom admire her bouquet. Before she had the chance to even eyeball my next gift—my spazzy self draped her in a pale pink, Miss America-style sash over her head—she looked down and read the silver glittery words displayed in all capital letters: "WE DID IT."

Based on her smile and the nodding of her head, I instantly knew that she understood the meaning behind the words. But that didn't stop me from refreshing her memory. Actually, maybe I needed to hear it again, as well as Christine and the patient sitting nearby.

"Remember the awful day of your diagnosis, when we stood in that parking lot, and you were crying out, saying you couldn't do it? I told you that you were right, you couldn't do it alone, but with God, you could. Right then, you changed your mind, Mom, showing everyone and even yourself that with God, all things are possible."

By then, the dam completely burst. Oblivious to our usual sensitivity toward other patients' feelings and interpretations, Mom and I stood there locked in a swaying hug, releasing months of pent-up relief and gratitude from our souls. I will never forget the intensity of the joyful whisper she kept repeating in my ear. To this day I still get the chills when I replay that scene in my head.

"Thank you, God. You are so good to me. Thank you. We did it! We did it."

Then, we fanned our faces and stifled our ugly cries. That meant it was time for business. I'm not kidding—once she sat down and was all hooked up, her treatment chair could've passed for a throne on top of a parade float. Mom looked like a pageant queen, smiling in her pink lipstick and waving to everyone who passed as they gave her a thumbs up or a hearty congratulations. I never thought that treatment room could hold such joy, but that day, it did.

For a short minute or two, as I managed to catch a few conscious breaths, I noticed something. It was something deeper than the average sense of deja vu. *How weird. This reminds me of when Mom gave me my comeback mum. The words, the glitter, the ribbon—it's different, yet the same in many ways.*

There we were again: the power of the moment mimicking similar emotions from the past.

Before I could fully grasp the revelation of this full-circle event, which would've probably brought me to tears again, Mom's impromptu question snapped me out of my trance. "So how do you think my hair will grow back? Straight or curly?"

I smiled, hearing her hope-filled question, visualizing her with straighter blonde hair than before. We sat there like giddy teenagers talking about new hairstyles and how she couldn't wait to get back in shape from the extra weight she had gained from the steroids. She was also going to join the church committee. (Side note: A few months after treatment, Mom's beautiful new wavy hair growth was tamed by an Annie Lennox style—not a trend that just any woman in her sixties could pull off.)

While listening to Mom plan her post-cancer to-do list, a wave of impatience came over me. I wanted so badly for those magic words written in bold print from the scan report "NO EVIDENCE OF CANCER" to instantly manifest themselves physically on my mom. It felt like forever since I had seen my mom's head full of hair, since I'd seen her energetic, happy go lucky, and faith-filled. One look at that sash brought me back to the reality that her hair and everything else would come back. *The same God who got Mom to this point of healing is the same God who's going to work out the rest. Be patient, Marla. Just be patient.*

Before I knew it, her treatment was over, and I was hiding near the side hallway, whispering on the phone as I strategically planned our exit. My aunts and cousin were patiently waiting outside the building.

While I was growing up, Mom used to tell me all the time, "Don't bother keeping things from me because I can read you like a book." For the most part, she was right. My whole life, no matter how hard I tried, she always could sense when something was up with me—with the exception of a few Academy Award-worthy performances by yours truly during my teenage years (and yes, I do admit a few in my adult years, too).

Hoping Mom wouldn't catch on to my little undercover stunt, once Christine finally unhooked her from her last IV bag, I went into full-fledged Best Actress in a Leading Role mode.

"Yay! All done." I hugged her. "Let's get the show on the road, shall we? I'm hungry. You hungry?"

I could tell Mom wanted to break free from what had become her home away from home over the past five months. Quickly, she gathered her purse and tote bag. "Yeah, let's go eat."

The medical staff gathered around her one last time, sending her off with hugs and well wishes and telling her what a great patient she was, while Mom thanked them for the umpteenth time. "Hope you never have to take care of me again," she joked.

At the time, I didn't realize the impact that my next decision was going to make on everyone in the room. I knew in my heart that it was Mom's turn to shine. I took her overstuffed purse and tote bag. "Here, let's lighten your load, I said. You just carry your flowers."

There was no protest like she'd normally give with that kind of command. She simply smiled, readjusted her sash, and took hold of her bouquet. What happened next felt like a scene from a documentary set in slow motion. Man, I wish I'd had a video camera. I'm not kidding when I say this, but Mom was glowing. Her face, her smile, and her aura radiated light. In the moment, I chalked it up to my imagination, but I now know it had to be something greater. It had to be the Holy Spirit.

All eyes were on Mom as she walked past the patients still sitting there hooked up to their lifelines. Perhaps they were attracted to her sash and flowers or the radiant glow coming from her body. Who knows? She barely made it past the first patient in the row of chairs before one pale-looking man asked her what her sash read. Mom's compassionate eyes locked into his and the other surrounding patients and family members, who all leaned in to hear her "WE DID IT" explanation. My heart swelled with pride as Mom tapped into their spirits, giving them hope and encouragement.

Of course, it didn't stop with that row of patients, not with my dynamic Mom. Try four more rows of the same thing. One minute she was walking down the aisle in Miss America fashion, and the next, she was "preparing the way" like John the Baptist for those lost and weary in their own deserts.

She was ministering left and right, offering her testimony of hope, thanksgiving, and trust in God. I was in so much awe that I didn't notice the time. I looked at my watch and noticed half an hour had gone since my "All clear, we're on our way" text message to my aunt.

Quickly and ever so nonchalantly, I escorted Mom toward the door like a secret service agent. Choking back tears in the crowded elevator, I couldn't help but visualize her next grand exit that was coming just a few floors down. I had a feeling it was going to be a doozy, and I was right. (We're all known to be sensitive and cry at the drop of a hat—but this was different.)

One step out the door and boom—Mom began to cry uncontrollably at the sight of seeing her two sisters and niece standing there holding their cards, flowers, and colorful balloons. All I remember was the overwhelming feeling when I witnessed Mom and her two sisters embracing and crying in a way I had never seen before. Mom was one of them now—a proud member of their breast cancer survivor club.

Our mission was accomplished. After we composed ourselves and noticed we were blocking the entrance to the building, we scooted ourselves off to the side for some picture-taking and Mom's balloon release. The whole time, she kept saying, "Oh, wow! You all didn't have to do this. It's so nice. Thank you." All eyes were on Mom, and she was beaming while passersby looked on with curious smiles.

Her surprise crew had her write down on a piece of paper whatever she wanted and attach it to her balloons. She cried some more as she jotted down her sacred thoughts before releasing them into the heavens.

As we watched her bouquet of balloons fly away, I couldn't help but notice her "WE DID IT" sash waving in the wind, reminding me once again of God's goodness and how far Mom had come.

My voice quivering, I began to clap, yelling "Yay, Mom!" over and over again. I felt like I wanted to cry, but I couldn't. There were no tears left—only joy. Cancer was behind us. It was time to celebrate and to live. And to eat.

Like me and my mum, my mother also kept her sash tacked to the hallway wall next to her favorite framed photos of the family—until the day we sold the house. Her sash now hangs on my desk shelf as a reminder of how special our full-circle moment was, and to remind me that with God, I can do anything.

Chapter 7

Love Is ... a Role Reversal

Love is caring about somebody,
Like a nurse making someone feel better.
When I grow up, I am going to be a nurse.
By being a nurse, you show you care.

—Marla Lozano, third grader

*M*y concept of love has evolved significantly over the years. I'm reminded of that simple fact every time I revisit memory lane, which I'm doing a lot these days, courtesy of pushing the big Five-O (AND writing a heartfelt memoir at the same time). Back in my childhood days, love meant being a full-fledged Mommy's girl, my first crush, favorite cartoons, and eating sweets. As a teen, it was another crush, being a lunatic Lionel Richie fan, talking on the phone, and eating chocolate. Then, young adulthood served me some fresh, more mature ideas on love. I learned about true love by marrying my college sweetheart, becoming a nurse and mother of four, and caring for my parents (all while still eating chocolate).

Of course, my love for God has always been the foundation of who I am. But now that I'm older, I'm seeing it through HIS eyes, making my definition of love stronger and broader. I'm even in the process of learning to love myself more, which, in itself, is a big deal. But in order to tell you how I got to a place of mature and broader love, I have to take you back to the time in my life where that all began.

My third grade teacher, Mrs. Rains, had us rest our heads on our desks for quiet time. Overachiever that I was, I made sure to keep perfectly still. Pleasing Mrs. Rains was always on my radar for two reasons: 1) she embodied the archetype of the strict, no-nonsense, high-standards teacher, and 2) she was friends with Mom.

I sat there with my head resting on my left arm while my right hand was in front of my face. I started to focus on the details of my hand, the creases in my pale skin, the shape of my fingers, and the way the fingers moved with a simple command in my mind. All of a sudden, I became fascinated by the three-dimensionality of my hand. The best way I can describe the way my hand looked is with the scene from *Back to the Future* when Michael J. Fox's character, Marty McFly, is on stage waiting for his parents to kiss. He kept looking at his hand, as it faded in and out because if his parents didn't kiss, he wouldn't exist. That's exactly what my hand looked like to me.

Right when my hand came back into focus, I thought to myself: *Why am I here? Why did God make me?* Looking back, I realize that was a pretty deep question for an eight-year-old to ask. My curiosity had gotten the best of me. As soon as I got home from school, I ran straight up to Mom and asked her the question that had been plaguing my thoughts all afternoon.

"Mom! Why am I here? Do you know why God made me?"

Without hesitation, as if she'd been preparing herself to answer this mind-blowing question her entire life, she sweetly smiled and replied, "You're here to love and serve God. That's why He made you."

As a third-grader, I was, of course, confused by her answer. "But I don't want to be a nun," I whined back. (I remembered her definition of a nun from years earlier.)

She laughed and tried to explain that I didn't have to be a nun. "You can love and serve God by caring for other people and showing His love to them." She started to spew out these long, drawn-out, meaning-of-life kinds of details that went WAY over my head. I felt like Peppermint Patty listening to her teacher: *Whaaaa, Whaaa. Whaaa.* None of it made any sense to me. I just nodded and then went outside to play. It would be a long time before I was ready to revisit that question.

That same year, I was assigned to do my first book report. I chose to read a biography on Florence Nightingale, the woman widely recognized as the founder of modern nursing. I don't remember what prompted me to choose her at the time, but in hindsight, I'm going to go ahead and call it Divine inspiration. It fascinated me to learn how the injured soldiers during the Crimean War called out to her, "Lady with the Lamp! Here she comes. Lady with the Lamp," as they lay there on the battlefield wounded and bleeding to death. With those intense scenes floating in my head, I realized that Florence Nightingale's passion for helping the sick and wounded soldiers was the epitome of loving and serving. After I finished that book report, there was no doubt in my mind: I wanted to be a nurse.

A few months after finishing that book report, I decided to enter the annual Cultural Arts Contest that my school district sponsored every year. There was always a theme, and students could write, act, draw, dance, or play a musical instrument to describe that theme. This particular year, the theme was: "Love Is."

I decided to write a poem for my entry. Don't ask me why. For the life of me, I still can't believe I chose to write a poem. I had always been a showgirl at heart. Dancing onstage for talent shows had been my thing since kindergarten, courtesy of Mom's homegrown seventies choreography skills. Always encouraging, she was probably relieved she didn't have to make up another dance routine. Mom rallied behind me as always, insisting I go for it and write my own interpretation of "Love Is."

Despite my lack of experience in the poetry department, the writing just flowed. Proud of my little poem, I approached Mom in a "ta da" fashion as I proudly handed her my verses scrawled on a sheet of notebook paper.

She beamed. I took a deep breath and suddenly felt a whole foot taller. In my eyes, it meant that my first official judge—the one whose opinion meant the world to me— was pleased with my work. Maybe Mom realized that the answer to my deep-seated question about the reason for my existence was unfolding right before our eyes.

"Wow, honey. That's good! I like it," she said before pausing. "Just don't forget to add a comma right there."

I should've known there would be more to follow from that initial light-hearted critique. Within a matter of seconds, Mom was cracking the whip. The rest of my afternoon was spent rewriting my poem, correcting my punctuation, making sure my cursive writing was impeccable, and that there were no erase marks to be seen. It had to be perfect. Mom was known for her outstanding penmanship during her high school days, and she made doggone sure I would follow her lead. And I did.

Hours later, shaking my writing hand to relieve the cramps from my overworked little fingers, I hovered over Mom while she evaluated what felt like my hundredth attempt at perfection. Once again, Mom was beaming.

"There. Much better. See how nice it looks?"

Receiving Mom's stamp of approval was all I needed to feel the satisfaction of a job well done. Winning first place in the school contest was just icing on the cake. But what really stands out in my memory is the pride I felt as I made the declaration to myself, to Mom, to the judges of the contest, and to everyone else who read my poem that day: I was going to be a nurse.

Fast forward to May of 1991. My dream of becoming a nurse had turned into a reality. I can't describe the relief I felt at having the stress of nursing school and clinical rotations behind me. I was so ecstatic that I went to the chapel on my last day just to thank God for getting me through. Mom was second on my list to thank. Humbled by my newfound freedom and gratitude, I called her on the phone, crying and thanked her for being my backbone, my cheerleader, my bank teller, and my spiritual prayer warrior. (Heaven only knows how many prayer intentions and rosaries she recited on my behalf.) I could tell by her joyful and surprised reaction that my acknowledgement of her contribution toward my success was music to her ears—that her once self-absorbed teenage daughter had finally learned mindfulness and appreciation of her mother's support. I bet Mom wished she had a tape recorder as I rattled off my laundry list of insightful accolades like a world-renowned auctioneer.

Just when I thought I had covered all the bases in the thank you department, Mom popped out yet another sign of maternal support in the most creative way. After my graduation party, once everybody had left, she handed me one last present while just the two of us were in her living room. She was beaming.

"Here you go. One last present for my little R.N."

I was caught off guard. "What? What's this? You and Dad already got me a gift."

Giddy, Mom replied, "I know, but this one's from *me!*"

I opened the box, and there was my LOVE IS poem mounted on yellow cardstock paper and perfectly displayed in a gold-trimmed picture frame.

"Oh, my God. You kept it all these years. Mother?!"

Talk about bawling—there we were in the same living room where I first wrote my poem thirteen years earlier, hugging and crying as we read and reflected on my little third-grade mission statement. Mom's treasure became my own. To this day, it hangs on my wall to remind me not only of Mom's love, but also that my life's purpose is being fulfilled—not to mention that dreams do come true.

Much to my nursing instructors' dismay, however, right after graduation, I headed straight to the Labor and Delivery Unit to work as a newbie R.N. (They advised all new grads to work at least a year on a medical/surgical floor before working in a special unit.) During my clinical rotations in nursing school, I discovered fast that

Labor and Delivery fit my personality. Don't laugh, but in a strange way, it brought out the high school cheerleader in me—minus the pom poms.

I simply enjoyed encouraging my patients and taking part in the miracle of life. Sure, there were intense and scary scenarios during my L&D clinicals, but nothing like I'd witnessed in other units. My sensitivity to seeing children who were sick, people suffering with chronic disease such as cancer, or patients facing death affected me on such a deep level. I'd come home from my rotations in other units drained, sad, or convinced I had the same symptoms as my patients.

One time, I went to the doctor thinking I had a vascular disease in my right breast—a condition I had observed in one of my older female patients. I had just gotten out of the shower and noticed a dark blue vein protruding from my breast. Panicked, I rushed to my gynecologist.

"I think I have the same breast disease as my patient," I cried. "Look at my breast. See it? It's right there."

The vein I was pointing to was so inconspicuous that he practically had to get out his magnifying glass to see it. In his happy-go-lucky Texan accent, Dr. Bolling kindly informed me that it was normal for a very pale, fair-skinned woman like me to see their veins dilate when hot water hits their skin. He diagnosed me with Medical Student Syndrome, a common condition in which we become sure we have the same diseases or symptoms as the patients we're studying.

Having been accurately diagnosed, I went on my merry way, relieved that I didn't have a diseased breast after all, that there was a name for my paranoia—and that I was simply not meant to care for sick, sick patients.

Keep it light, Marla. Keep it happy. You aren't meant to be the kind of nurse who works with the sick and dying patients. It isn't your forte. Always remember that about yourself.

Those were the beliefs I bestowed on myself during my last semester of nursing school, and I maintained that mindset all the way up to the fifteen-year mark of my Labor and Delivery career.

It's interesting how in 2005, God chose to broaden my scope of practice and challenge my self-beliefs by assigning me two VIPs in the form of my cancer-stricken parents. First, it was Dad's bladder cancer, and a year later, it was Mom's breast cancer. With each passing chemo treatment, hospitalization, and medical scan came numerous prayers that gave me the inner strength of knowing I could handle the non-L&D side of nursing.

Then, the big challenge came. It was only a few months after Dad died that we discovered Mom's cancer was back. This time the tumor was in her brain. A four-centimeter tumor located in the cerebellum had to be removed.

Considering she'd undergone major brain surgery, Mom handled the recovery process quite well. I wish I could say the same for myself.

"We've got to wash your hair Mom. Look at that!" I said, carefully picking off dried blood and adhesive remnants stuck to her head and neck. I was using my fake enthusiastic voice. "Come on over here, Mom. Let's wash your hair. You ready?"

Mom's Vicodin-induced response was a flat, "Okay, I'm ready."

It was one of those "Don't ever let them see you sweat" moments. I was determined not to let Mom see me sad—sad from missing Dad and sad from missing my healthy Mom. I was running on fumes of adrenaline and grief. Time stood still as I slowly guided Mom's fragile head and body to lean over my kitchen sink.

I had a sick feeling inside, knowing it was going to be a challenge as I carefully examined the freshly-healed sutured line on her head. Determined to make this experience a positive one, though, I began to reflect on our sweet hair-washing ritual from my childhood days. She would stand by the kitchen sink waiting for me as I juggled the big bottles of Wella Balsam shampoo and conditioner in my tiny arms, with the weight of a terry cloth towel draped over my shoulder. I'd assume the position, standing on a chair, bent over with my head in the sink, ready for my mini spa treatment to begin. It was *my* reward for the torturous detangling sessions that always occurred just minutes earlier. Each excruciating session included a crying spell by yours truly, along with the added bonus of Mom's frustrated murmurs of the words "rat's nest" and "stay still."

In an instant, the drama of it all was erased as soon as I dipped my head in the sink. It felt like heaven. Mom's touch was soft and her demeanor calm as she sweetly imitated Goldilocks, asking, "Is the water too hot? Does this feel too cold?" She carefully adjusted the temperature until it was just right.

After the final rinse, Mom towel-dried my soppy hair and wrapped it in a turban-style twist. "There. All done. Muuuah!" Her kisses always included an auditory component.

Her standard quick peck on the lips followed by her tender hug became the usual finale of our sweet bonding moments. There was so much love involved in our many hair-washing sessions that I secretly wished I could stay little so that Mom could be my permanent hair-washer.

Now, here I was in total role reversal mode, sharing the same techniques she once used with me and mimicking the calm reassuring voice she used to speak to me. "Is the water too hot?" I asked.

"It's fine, honey." Still flat.

"Okay, Mom, keep your head down; don't move. Don't want to get soap in your eyes." I used a small cup to rinse those hard to reach places. Her petite body was starting to tremble as she tried to hold her head still.

"Here, Mom. Just let your head drop into my hand, and relax." My hand supported her head while the other did the rinsing. "Almost done, Mom. You are doing good!"

That was when I started to cry. Her hearing aids were off, and the water was running. So I didn't have to worry that she could hear me. My tears became liquid prayers as I begged God to heal her brain.

Then, all of a sudden, I felt this peace—a familiar feeling that I recognize from God. I heard in my heart, "Marla, use my water."

The straightforward instruction led my eyes to the Holy Water bottle sitting on the opposite side of the sink. Mom had given me that Holy water from my parents' pilgrimage to the Holy Land back in 2007. I quickly grabbed the bottle and added a few drops to her head. God's peaceful presence surrounded us. Mom was no longer shaking, and I was no longer crying. I began to make Sign of the Cross motions tenderly over her head while rinsing off the rest of the shampoo.

"There you go, Mom. All done." I gently wrapped the lightweight terry cloth towel turban-style over her head and sealed it with a quick peck on the lips.

Mom's eyes lit up. "Thank you, honey. That felt good!"

I smiled with relief, "You're welcome, Momma." It was another full-circle moment that led me to repeat to God what Mom had just said.

"Thank you, God. That felt good."

After my thanksgiving dialogue with God, I couldn't help but reflect on my third-grade mission statement that was hanging on my wall just a few feet away. It all made sense. It was a spiritual aha and full-circle moment all rolled into one. Overjoyed at having just experienced another dimension of what love is, I thought to myself: *If there would ever be an adult Cultural Arts Contest, I would write an updated version of my poem. It would go something like this:*

Love is caring about somebody,
Like a nurse, making someone feel better.
I grew up and became a nurse.
By being a nurse and daughter, I showed I cared and made my mom feel better.
—Marla Lackey, forty-six-year-old

1975 *This photo was taken right before my first dance recital at the tender age of six. Mom's arms and lap had always been my safety net, and that was just what I needed to relieve my jitters.*

1986 *Not only was this my Varsity comeback year, but it was also the year my mom became my biggest cheerleader.*

2006 *Introducing my very bald, bold, brave and beautiful parents, Robert and Sandra Lozano. Despite the sadness and vulnerability that surrounded that day, Mom later confessed that this picture was one of her favorites.*

2006 *This was Mom's last day of chemo. As you can see Mom (a.k.a. Miss America) and I were about to burst with relief and gratitude. It was beautiful to experience the full-circle moment of becoming Mom's cheerleader the same way she had been mine.*

2007 *My siblings, Mark and Monica, and I honored our rock-star by participating in the annual Race for the Cure walk. I'm not sure who was more proud that day—we, as her children, or Mom, who always cherished being with us at the same time.*

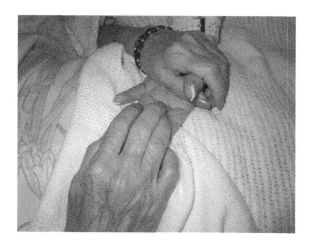

2010 *Every mother knows her child's voice. Days before Mom passed away, while in a comatose state, she reached her arm out to touch my hand. This was our last form of communication. It may have been nonverbal, but that made it no less powerful.*

Chapter 8

Sunrise, Sunset

"No way, Mom. I am *not* playing this song at my wedding."

The year was 1992, and I was just six months shy of tying the knot with my then-fiancé, Mike. I sat in the passenger's seat of Mom's car duking it out with her over every trivial nuptial detail. Of course, when it's your wedding, every decision is life and death, including the music to be played during the ceremony. (As I write this book, I'm proud to say that Mike and I will soon celebrate our twenty-fifth wedding anniversary.)

Wedding planning with Mom felt much like wardrobe shopping with her during my teen years. She felt the exact opposite of every one of my choices and opinions. So when I told her I wanted to play some Lionel Richie songs during the ceremony (of course), she was armed and ready with an entirely different selection.

"'Sunrise, Sunset' is a beautiful song, Marla. It has so much meaning."

I wasn't convinced. "It's an old song and sounds way too cheesy, and besides, I've never even seen *Fiddler On the Roof.*"

"Well, then, maybe you should."

Mom was a lifelong enthusiast of musical theater, and *Fiddler on the Roof* was one of her favorite musicals. It's about a proud and strict father who struggles emotionally when three of his five daughters break with tradition when it's time for them to marry.

In the "Sunrise, Sunset" scene during the marriage of one of the daughters, the parents sing the song, which reflects on the fast passing of time as they've watched their children grow up.

Naturally, Mom took this opportunity to dramatically narrate the scene for me in painstaking detail, even getting genuinely choked up toward the end. She concluded her spiel with the classic line, "One day when you're a parent, you'll understand."

In the back of my mind, I knew where she was coming from. She had always been the reflective, sentimental type. But in that moment, my inner bridezilla was still holding the reins. We went back and forth—for longer than I care to admit—until Mom whipped out the ultimate trump card: "Besides, who's paying for this wedding anyway?"

Dead silence always seemed to follow this strategic question. It was a tactic I knew all too well. I held my breath the same way I did as a teenager anytime I had to negotiate a piece of clothing she thought was inappropriate or a curfew she thought was too late. But recognizing my imminent defeat, I finally gave in and let my guard down.

I grimaced. Mom grinned. She knew her battle had been won.

As so it was. The song "Sunrise, Sunset" permeated the walls of the church along with everyone's hearts while the beaming mother of the bride practically floated down the church aisle to light her side of the unity candle.

It wasn't until much later—when I became a mother myself—that I finally understood the sentiment behind that song. It resonates with me more and more as time goes on, just like Mom said it would. To this day, I still can't listen to "Sunrise, Sunset" without getting a little choked up. As much as Mom tried to prepare me for the challenges of life, what she didn't prepare me for was just how personally significant the title of that song would become as I transitioned into the role of her caregiver and watched the changes that took over her body toward the end of her life.

For most of her life, Mom just wasn't a morning person—a genetic trait that she apparently passed on to me. She was never the type to get up at the crack of dawn and sit outside admiring the sunrise over a cup of coffee. For her, waking up at 10:00 a.m., 11:00 a.m., or sometimes noon was the norm on her days off, and the rest of the family usually followed suit—everyone except Dad, that is.

Most Saturday mornings/afternoons, he'd barge into their bedroom and interrupt Mom's peaceful slumber with his half-joking, half-annoyed wisecrack: "You're gonna sleep half your life away. Wake up."

She'd moan, turn over in bed, and quickly answer, "Five more minutes," which, in reality, meant fifteen or thirty minutes, sometimes even longer. Dad was like her personal alarm clock set on snooze, going in and out of the bedroom in exasperation. I'd cringe at the sound of him trying to wake her up, knowing I was next in line for a less-than-gentle wake-up call.

His comments never seemed to phase her, though, and for most of her life, Mom continued to succumb to her own natural circadian rhythm, which suited her just fine. But her affinity for sunsets was more than just a feature of her biological clock. She was in tune with them on an almost spiritual level. It was a connection that transcended the superficial aesthetic appeal of an orange and purple sky.

During the summer months, Mom and I could usually be found outside in the evenings as the sun was setting. If we weren't making laps around the high school running track, we'd be out in the yard tending to her plants or watering the grass. Her daily observation on the beauty of the sunset was as good as guaranteed. The sight of the blazing sky just as the sun dipped below the horizon never ceased to amaze her. "Wow, look at that sky!" she would say, and you could hear the genuine wonder in her voice.

And there's something else I always noticed with Mom. As far back as I can remember, she was that woman who always had a camera around to capture monumental moments, celebrations, and even our everyday events that seemed routine and mundane (at least back then). But to her, it was exciting. Her family was her world. When we were kids, it was a Kodak pocket camera with the old-school flash cube on top. Later, she was thrilled to upgrade to a compact point and shoot camera that allowed her to snap infinitely more photos—most of which depicted candid moments with the grandkids.

I have stumbled across tons of photos of sunsets that she took. Hawaii was Mom and Dad's go-to vacation spot, and she captured some breathtaking images of the sun setting over the Pacific Ocean.

Sunsets meant something different during the fall season, when we'd have to change our clocks back an hour. "Man, it seems so late, already. I don't like it getting dark so early," Mom would say with a yawn. It was her nightly mantra throughout the months of Daylight Savings Time.

If she wasn't attending any evening activities, she could almost certainly be found wearing her comfy velour sweats, curled up in her recliner, and covered beneath her cozy afghan. She was done for the day, even though it was only 6:00 p.m. I could never understand why she had difficulty with the time change. For many consecutive years in a row (mostly teenage years) I'd roll my eyes and think to myself: *Really? What's the big deal? It's only* one *hour back.*

Nevertheless, no matter how pumped up I was from cheerleading practice or a game, I seemed to get in a hypnotic state of coziness once I got home and saw Mom ready for bed. Every once in a while, I conformed to her early evening routine and snuggled up with her as we lay on opposite sides of the couch, covered by her homemade afghan and watching our favorite eighties episodes of *Dynasty* and *Dallas.*

A sense of calm and safety always seemed to seep through the holes of that afghan. What was Mom talking about? Daylight Savings Time, early sunsets, cozy nights.

It took a semester in nursing school, a season of watching my maternal grandmother's cognitive decline, and multiple episodes of caring for Mom to grasp the whole concept of how one simple sunset can affect someone's whole being.

During my time in nursing school, I had a critical care rotation that required me to work in the ICU. One evening, I came back from my dinner break, shocked to find my formerly sweet, alert, and well-oriented elderly patient in an agitated and confused state. She no longer knew who I was. Right away, I rushed to the nurse who had been following her during my break.

"What happened to her while I was gone?" I asked. "Did someone give her a wrong med or something?"

The nurse chuckled and answered nonchalantly (in the way some veteran nurses do with newbie students), "Nah, she's just sundowning."

I'm sure she could tell by the look on my face that I hadn't gotten that so-called sundowning chapter in school. I have to admit, it freaked me out to see someone's mental status change so drastically. I was young. I was naive. I had so much to learn.

The official name for it is Sundown Syndrome. It's a condition that's typically characterized by the onset of confusion and restlessness in response to the sun setting. Sundown Syndrome tends to affect the elderly, as well as people who suffer from dementia or other forms of cognitive impairment.

After nursing school, I watched my maternal grandmother, Nana, experience the same symptoms as my ICU patient during an overnight stay in the hospital. Mom tried to warn me, "Now, remember, your Nana may get really confused during the night and try to get out of bed, so just watch out, okay?"

The nurse side of me was prepared for the task at hand, but the granddaughter side lagged behind, worried over seeing my beloved Nana disoriented, fretful, and rambling. It was going to be a long night.

After those experiences with my patient during nursing school and with my own grandmother, I was familiar enough with Sundown Syndrome to recognize the signs. So as soon as Mom started exhibiting similar symptoms, I knew where it was headed.

In 2010, the brain surgery to remove Mom's cancerous tumor, the whole brain radiation, and the insertion of a brain shunt all wreaked havoc with her vibrant mind. Her yearly Daylight Savings Time mantra during the eighties had now become my mantra. I would've given anything to go back in time to feel the tranquility of cuddling up next to her on the couch—the unofficial signal that our day was coming to a close. Instead, I had to witness her shift into a world of anxiety and confusion.

The heaviness in my heart couldn't keep up with the rapid pace of Mom's cognitive and motor decline. Before I knew it, she was on the verge of being discharged from the hospital into home hospice.

I'm proud to report that despite the ugly truth staring me in the face, I remained positive—at least around Mom. As I cared for her one night, it was hard to avoid the feeling that the drab-colored walls and faded artwork in her room were going to cave in on me. So I focused on the vibrant and colorful pictures of Jesus and Mother Mary that I had taped on the wall near the foot of her bed. They gave me the spiritual boost I needed to pray and stay in sync with my faith.

Naturally, the TV was on in her room. Heaven forbid there would be silence. I'm not ashamed to admit that my family grew up as TV junkies. Back when programs were actually entertaining, the television set was our babysitter, comforter, and distractor. Like clockwork, Pat Sajak's and Vanna White's waves of goodbye each evening never failed to synchronize with the sunset.

Before Mom's nurse entered her room to distribute her scheduled meds, I half-jokingly asked the same question frequently asked by my patients' family members: "Wouldn't happen to have any extra Xanax there for me, would you?"

We were in for a long night. The combination of sundowning, side effects of pain and anti-anxiety medication, plus being in the hospital would only exacerbate Mom's already fragile and sleep-deprived state. Thankfully, a few late visits from family and medical staff delayed the experience of watching her enter her own world.

Preparing Mom for bed, I silently begged, *Oh, God, please let Mom have a good night. She needs to rest. Please help her. And help me.* I gently patted her legs, bent down, and sealed my heartwarming gesture with a hug and kiss. "There you go, Mom. All tucked in, nice and cozy." I wasn't sure if my fake, happy-go-lucky voice cancelled out my inner desperation. She always said she could read me like a book.

It must have worked, though, because she smiled as she recognized the same bedtime ritual she used with me. "Goodnight, honey." Her reply was strikingly coherent. Such simple words. So familiar. So Mom. Determined to savor the moment, I let her sweet, oriented response soak in.

Within minutes, she was out like a light. Guided by the glow peeking through the slit of the bathroom door, I carefully tiptoed my way to the foldout cot next to her bed. Covered up and cozy as one can get on a hospital cot, I thanked God for blessing us with a good night thus far.

As soon as my head hit the pillow, however, Mom began to stir. I immediately reacted in my head. *Aww, man! Come on, God. I just finished thanking you for blessing us, begged you for a good night's sleep, and now this?*

Feeling frustrated, I glanced over to find Mom's restlessness and confusion starting to rev up. She was trying to get out of bed. I reoriented her with a whisper. "Go back to sleep, Mom. You're in the hospital. I'm right here. It's okay."

Oh, how I wished the dimly lit room had been dark enough to hide the look of fear and confusion on her face because it broke my heart. She responded with a sweet, "Okay, honey."

The tucking in process would start over and over and over again. I just wanted my poor tired mother to sleep. *I wanted to sleep, too.* My threshold was now lowered after two to three hours of what I call our version of the movie, *Groundhog Day*.

No amount of reassurance from the night shift nurses about the "normalcy" of it all helped me. "Don't worry," one of them said. "We see this all the time in our older patients."

I wanted to scream in her face, "Duh. I know that! But this is *my* mother we're talking about. And who are you calling elderly? Not *my* mom. Can't you see this is torture for both of us? I just want her to sleep, damn it."

Based on her empathetic response, she must've been telepathic. "I know it's hard seeing her like this. Let me see about another med to help her sleep."

The nurse in me was looking for every avenue to make it better—to no avail. It was starting to become unsafe as I caught myself dozing off while Mom was trying to get out of bed. The night shift nurse suggested using padded restraints to help her stay in bed.

My defensive, knee-jerk reaction was, "No way am I going to have my Momma tied down to a bed. Not on my watch. No way, no how."

Within the following hour, Mom had gotten up so many times while I was dozing off that I was now concerned that she would fall and break a hip. I was a hot mess. Guilt and desperation took over, guiding me to finally agree to the padded restraints.

"It's okay," her nurse reassured me, as she carefully applied each restraint. "Sometimes, we have to do these things to keep them safe."

I turned my face away so that Mom couldn't see me cry. "Please, God, let this work. Help her go back to sleep!"

Unfortunately, my prayer this time went unanswered. After thirty minutes of what seemed like hours, I decided to put the restraints away and rely on God to get us through this all-nighter.

My mind went back to the stories and memories of how Mom used to hold me all day or night when I was a sick baby, lying down with me in bed and ready to help me to the bathroom. She did the same with my own children. She would often retell the story of how during her pregnancy, carrying an almost nine-pound Marla, she used to sleep on the floor to help relieve pressure from her achy back. I kept her up before I was even born! I told myself that this is the least I could do in return for her sacrifice.

Yet another beautiful full-circle moment was revealing itself, allowing me to become aware of and accept this sacred time. Restraints off and with a renewed outlook,

I suggested, "Come on, Mom. You can stand up. I'll hold you for as long as you want." A second wind came over both of us, which I now know was the Holy Spirit.

Even though she seemed more alert, more talkative, and a little less confused, her body trembled. I couldn't tell if the culprit was her anxiety or the common side effects of the meds. Firmly holding her in my arms turned into a slow dance of swaying back and forth to our own silent rhythm. The moonlight shining through the blinds made it easier to see her delicate facial features. Our eyes met, and I saw fear.

"I … I'mmmm scccaaared, Mmaaarrlaa. Heellp mmee! Pleaase ppray ffor mmee!"

I wanted to cry, but I held it together. Without hesitation, in the same way a mother distracts their distraught child with a toy, I reached for my new rosary. "Look, Mom! Look at this rosary my friend, Mary, brought for me all the way from Ireland. Isn't it beautiful? Feel the shape of the beads. Look at this Celtic cross!"

Mom lit up. "Wow! Look at that." Treasuring her deep-rooted Catholic faith was something she took seriously. "How about we pray the Rosary?" It was Mom's second language.

We prayed our Hail Marys and Our Fathers in unison as we continued to sway back and forth. Her legs, once trembling, were now steady, and her body was totally relaxed. We swayed, prayed, and sang church songs from the past and present, with even modern-day songs from my kids' Bible videos.

We were on a roll—a roll of pure peace. God's perfect answer to my prayer helped lull Mom and I to sleep for the next four hours.

As the day shift nurse woke Mom up for her morning vitals, I went over to the window. And there it was: a sunrise. "Look at the sunrise, Momma. Isn't it beautiful?"

Without covering up her head or rolling over to try to go to sleep, Mom sat right up and smiled, "It sure is, honey."

She was back—even if it was just for a short while. *She was back.*

With full gratitude swelling up inside me, I kissed her forehead as a seal for her clarity, her love, and the spiritual bond we had shared the night before.

Chapter 9

Pep Rally

The crowd went wild. "We got spirit, yes we do! We got spirit; how about you!?!"

Our voices couldn't get any louder. As seniors, we had to keep the tradition going and win the spirit contest ... or else. With the veins popping out of our necks, trying fiercely to out-yell our classmates across the gym floor during our pep rallies, we were a few heartbeats away from a collective brain aneurysm. But we didn't care.

That was how we rolled in the eighties. School spirit ran high in those days. It was a sweet time in history when cell phones and social media weren't around to interrupt the excitement and energy of a winning football game or a rowdy pep rally. Totally in tune with what was going on around us, we all screamed, laughed, danced, and cheered our hormone-driven bodies to the brink of exhaustion. Back then, we were a force to be reckoned with. Just thinking about it still gives me goosebumps.

I had always been proud of my role as a cheerleader, especially with my new badge of honor as a comeback

119

kid. Even though I took my role very seriously, my goofy side took over from time to time. One funky beat from the drumline was all it took to get me in the zone and dance like nobody was watching—a sight that caused my slightly amused fan club (a.k.a. my parents) to shake their heads in embarrassment.

On top of being a cheerleader my senior year, I was also the student body president. It was a role I took seriously, yet still found to be fun. With a level of enthusiasm rivaling that of the spazzy cheerleader, Patty Simcox in *Grease*, I bebopped around campus, waving my pompoms and spreading school spirit. Outwardly, I may have appeared oblivious with a tad of ADHD, but beneath the surface, my soul was on a secret mission to capture every highlight of my senior year as best I could. *Don't forget, Marla: You're never going to be in high school again. Make the best of it. Enjoy! You're only young once.*

This tendency toward sensitivity wasn't new to me. Even as a young child, it wasn't unusual for me to cry at inopportune moments. I still remember sitting in the back seat of Mom's Ford LTD and holding back tears to as I listened to my mother's favorite eight-track tape of "The Carpenters."

"Isn't this a nice song?" Mom asked, cranking up the volume to Karen Carpenter belting out her hit, "We've Only Just Begun."

"Listen to that. She has the voice of an angel," Mom added.

Worried that she would notice the lump in my throat, I remained silent as I nodded abruptly and turned my head toward the window. It was confusing to me that I could experience such a powerful reaction when I barely even understood the meaning of the lyrics.

As with any mother who has tapped into her child's emotions, I'm sure Mom could sense my delicate responses to certain songs, no matter how hard I tried to hide them. She could have easily called me out in those moments when I inadvertently let my vulnerability show, but she didn't. Instead, she kept quiet and allowed me to discover for myself that I was just as sensitive as she was.

However, there were a few times when Mom couldn't help but take it upon herself to expedite the development of my self-awareness. I called it nagging. It annoyed me so much in the weeks leading up to my senior year. It didn't matter where we were—back to school shopping, getting paperwork squared away for registration, or sitting at the dinner table. When Mom blurted out in a loving tone, "Aww, I can't believe my Tinky is a 'senior,' my eye roll response made her even more adamant. "You'd better make the most of this year, you hear me? It's gonna fly by before, you know. Don't you look at me like that. I know what I'm saying. Trust me."

She didn't understand that my look came from a place of not just annoyance, but confusion. *Why does she have to remind me? Gah! I already know that.* Didn't she realize that I was still that sensitive girl? Even more

121

sensitive than ever before? After everything we had been through during my *Extreme Makeover: Varsity Edition*, I was well-versed in the gratitude department. So why was she still second-guessing my outlook?

Now, as a mother myself, I realize her stern reminder may have come from a place of fear that one day I might lose sight of my true self-identity. She didn't need to worry. My overly sensitive heart was already headed in that direction, ready to absorb and appreciate "the lasts" that were about to come my way.

As a result, I savored everything—the rowdy raw energy of a morning pep rally, the nail-biting suspense of a football game in overtime, the strictly enforced "no shoes allowed" policy that overshadowed every school dance in our stinky gym, and even the sweet relief of somehow flying under my parents' radar after getting busted for cheating on an algebra final. My list could go on and on. Then, of course, there were the handsome young men who escorted me to class, carrying my books when I had to walk on crutches after a cheerleading injury—you can bet I savored that!

There is one highlight, however, that stands out from all the others—one that still gives me goosebumps to this day. That highlight was performing with my cheer squad at our annual night pep rally.

This particular event was a far cry from our typical Friday morning pep rallies, where the less-than-enthusiastic McCollum Cowboys would haphazardly line up against the gym wall in their football jerseys while we cheerleaders would drag ourselves onto the center of the basketball court for our performance. Usually, the rest of the sleep-deprived student body relied on the drumline to perk them up like a shot of espresso. But nope; this was a pep rally on steroids. It always happened on the Thursday (a school night, which was a big deal back then) before the big homecoming game against our rival school, the Harlandale Indians.

The night pep rally was the one time during the year when practically the whole student body crammed itself into the school gym like sardines, alongside parents, faculty, and alumni. It was also the only day of the year when school administrators were amenable enough to look the other way as we lit up the celebratory bonfire. And then, there were the die-hard rule-breakers (present company excluded, obviously, with the exception of my algebra final faux pas), who saw their opportunity to push the envelope a little further than usual. These shenanigans included painting the street in front of our school and "decorating" our rival school's campus with broken eggs.

The vibration of the wooden gym floor under my feet from the drumline and band was intense. The sheer enthusiasm and sensory overload took me back to the adrenaline rush of my comeback cheerleader tryouts, when my jumps were so high that I practically hit the ceiling. The crowd roared so loud that I couldn't even hear our head cheerleader kick off our routines with her usual,

"Ready? Okay!" Masking every ounce of panic with a frozen smile, I threw out as many silent Hail Marys and Our Fathers in my head as I could in the hopes of not messing up. And it seemed to help. I only had a few minor glitches that, uncharacteristically, didn't get to me.

But with the pep rally's grueling roster of events, a few mistakes were inevitable. There were countless wardrobe changes for crazy skits, followed by a kick-ass, *Grease*-inspired senior dance routine, and a packed lineup of pep talks from those silent stud football players who normally didn't say a word. Then, to top it all off, there was the explosive fanfare of the annual bonfire, with students past and present yelling at the top of their lungs with aneurysm-inducing levels of adrenaline.

I was bound and determined to soak in every snippet of that powerful night, but there was one moment that stood out from the rest. It happened during one of the more challenging parts of my cheer routine—the one I had practiced countless times in front of my mother's full-length bedroom mirror, as Mom would critique. "Watch your arms. It doesn't look sharp enough. Try again."

Right then, I looked up into the crowded stands, and like a game of "Where's Waldo," I spotted my parents. It all happened so fast. Normally, when I saw my parents in the audience during a performance, I would look away to avoid becoming distracted. But this time, it was different. Comfortable and more focused than ever, I was able to capture the moment like a snapshot. I couldn't help but notice my dad grinning as he admired the sharp, synchronized movements of our fast-paced routine. Then, in the blink of an eye, my attention went straight to Mom.

Time suddenly stood still. Our eyes locked, and for the first time, I wasn't annoyed or distracted by seeing her in the stands. It's a good thing I wasn't because I saw Mom discreetly mouthing the words and mimicking the motions of our routine. Seeing the look of pride on her face made me feel like I was the only cheerleader performing that night. Soaking in every ounce of faith she had in me, I zoomed through the challenging part of the routine confidently and without a hitch. As we struck our final poses, glowing with exhilaration (and a thin layer of sweat), the crowd roared—but I swear, I could only hear Mom.

Leaving the gym in a state of total euphoria, my friends and I couldn't help but rehash the details of that magical night. As we walked toward our cars, a wave of sadness rolled over me. It occurred to me that I had just completed yet another "last" of my senior year of high school. But I wasn't ready to come to terms with that reality just yet. Tucking that realization deep into my soul, I quickly bounced back into the moment at hand. "This was the best pep rally EVER!" I declared. And I believed it.

Little did I know that in just twenty-four short years, that pep rally would be blown out of the water by an entirely different kind of rally.

"Don't worry," the hospice nurse reassured me. "I'm sure your mom will rally soon." Her words coated my heart with hope as I sat next to Mom's bedside, devastated at the sight of her fading away before my eyes.

Thanks to my medical background and the recent passing of my dad, I knew what the nurse was talking about. She was referring to an occurrence that hospice workers call an end-of-life rally, a short period of time when a dying patient's decline suddenly and inexplicably seems to reverse. They experience a surge of energy, uncharacteristically interested in walking, talking, eating, and engaging in lucid conversations with others. A year earlier, my family and I got to witness that phenomenon when my dad went from lying on his deathbed to sitting in a golf cart watching his grandson play golf. It was absolutely fascinating to see that second wind of energy and clarity take over during those couple of days. It felt like the miraculous scene from the Bible when Lazarus rose from the dead. As a family, we all knew better than to take the gift of Dad's rally for granted. Within two months, he went home to heaven.

Knowing that my Mom was an overachiever, I expected her to outdo my dad's rally by a thousand. It had been three days since she had been discharged from her final hospital stay to home hospice. She could barely walk, talk, or eat. When she did talk, it was only a few words at a time. Some of her words made sense; some didn't. Blank stares became the norm, and no matter how hard I tried, I couldn't help but yearn for the chance to see her be herself again—even if only for a minute.

While juggling the demands of tending to her physical needs, coordinating visits from friends and family, and preparing for the funeral, I often caught myself obsessing over the nurse's comment. I found myself praying for and even fantasizing about what Mom's rally would be like. Would she sit up and hold a coherent, reflective conversation with me? Would she smile, look me in the eye, and tell me she loved me? Would she embrace me with one of her signature spontaneous yet meaningful hugs, making me feel like all was right with the world? Would we witness her seeing my dad, her beloved parents, or even Jesus and his Mother Mary? The more she appeared to wither away, the more hopeful and sometimes outlandish my made-up scenarios became.

All that pent-up anticipation inside of me came to a head one cloudy and cold afternoon. As Mom's morning dose of morphine wore off, she woke up to a handful of people—my brother and sister, two aunts, a close cousin, and myself—standing over her bed, praying and singing her favorite church hymns. When we noticed her beginning to stir, I stopped and began talking to her. I kissed her dry, balm-coated lips and caressed her head.

"Well, hello there, Momma." I couldn't hide the surprise in my voice.

Her eyes met mine in the same loving way when she would wake me up from a deep sleep when I was a little girl.

She scanned the room, smiled, and proceeded to get out of bed with intention. As she got up, she exhibited full strength and range of motion, which we hadn't seen from her in weeks. Caught off guard by her Lazarus moment, we all jolted toward her.

Assuming the morphine was playing tricks on her body, I rushed to guide her upright. "Where are you going, Momma?"

Without skipping a beat, she nonchalantly replied, "To the kitchen. I'm going to get something to eat." Mom was on a mission, and there was no stopping her as she moved toward the edge of the bed.

"Let me get the wheelchair since you can't walk." I tried to sound calm and keep myself from freaking out.

I could tell she was starting to get annoyed with me. "No, I got it, I got it," she said, shooing me away with not only her hand but with the tone of her voice.

Everyone was blown away by her sudden burst of energy and clarity.

Despite her protests, my husband, Mike, got the wheelchair ready as I tried to coax her into it, "Okay, Mom, go ahead and get in the chair."

That was when I knew she was *really, really* back, because she gave me "the look." She didn't speak, but her eyes said it all: *What did I just say? Get away!*

Luckily, Mike was there to save the day. "Here, why don't you try this?" he sweetly interjected. He gently guided her hand to the back of the wheelchair for her to hold onto the handles so that she could use it like a walker. Her known adoration for her son-in-law resurfaced as she took his suggestion with grace.

"Oh, my God! Look at you, Mom. You're walking!" Guarding every slow and steady step she took, I knew in my gut that this was the moment I had been waiting for.

With a sweet grin and a look of sheer determination, Mom walked effortlessly down the hallway while her fan club followed behind, clapping and cheering her way as she turned two corners and made it to the kitchen unscathed.

The rest of us made our way into the kitchen as the miracle we had just witnessed began to set in. Still wide-eyed with awe, my brother, Mark, offered to make Mom her favorite sautéed spinach. She looked content, sitting at the table and engaging in conversation with us. She even offered glimpses of her old self with witty remarks about "being doted over" and gratitude for her surprise lunch.

I can't begin to describe the joy I experienced at the sight of Mom not just walking and talking, but feeding herself without any help. No spills from her cup. Not even a drop of spinach from her spoon. Her coordination and her awareness were both on point. We all beamed. Who could blame us? It was magical.

After she ate, I was determined to match Mom's outward appearance with the beauty that was emanating from within her soul. "Hey, Mom. How about I fix your hair and help you put some makeup on?" I asked.

She nodded and quickly took her last sip of soda. Ironically, there was no shooing me away at that suggestion. No matter how obstinate Mom was feeling, she could never turn down a beauty session.

Nestled snugly in her wheelchair, she appeared robust and sturdy. I couldn't believe how well she carried herself, holding her head upright and maintaining an even posture that I hadn't seen from her in months.

I began to brush the tiny tangles out of her wispy white hair. With each stroke of the brush, she appeared to morph back into the old Mom—the version of her that I still saw when I pictured her in my mind's eye. The light coming from her beautiful hazel eyes was undeniable. I wanted to crawl on her lap like a little girl, wrap my arms around her, and shout, *There you are! Oh, Mommy, I've missed you.* But instead, I kept on brushing, hiding my overwhelm behind countless compliments of how pretty her hair looked.

After I applied a subtle shimmering beige eyeshadow over her hooded eyelids and a hint of blush to her sallow cheeks, she perked up even more. She glanced at her makeup bag and asked, "Where's my lipstick?"

Before I could reach it, the lipstick queen herself slowly grabbed her tube of L'Oreal Mica #620 and began to apply it on her lips all on her own—no mirror needed. Surprisingly, it was flawless.

Looking radiant, happy, and more alert than ever before, Mom made her way to the bay window that overlooked her front yard. It was there that the Grand Finale took place. Sitting patiently in her wheelchair, she lit up on a whole new level as she watched all eight of her grandchildren walk up the sidewalk. Once inside, her precious jewels greeted her one by one with a hug and kiss, and she recognized each of them by the correct name, followed by her well-known animated Mimi kiss and a loud *MUAHHH!* Everything about that moment felt like old times.

Ever so grateful, I would tuck that special moment in time deep inside my soul, right alongside the memory of that special senior year pep rally all those years ago. But this time, it was about more than just preserving a memory; it was an homage honoring Mom's timeless lesson of "lasts."

I was wrong that night in high school. Mom's rally was actually the "best pep rally *ever.*" Her living room became like the gym. Her couch became the bleachers. Representing the student body were the small group of family members who came to cheer her on to the next life through their love and tears. Much like the students' cheers and chants, our prayers echoed loud and clear, with Mom unexpectedly chiming in from time to time. We also represented the cheerleaders and drill team, holding the momentum of those last sacred moments with our physical touch and words of faith. Singing hymns at her bedside, our voices quivering with every lyric, reminded me of the way our senior class sounded when we sang our *Alma Mater* for the last time that night so many years before. Mom's favorite CDs playing in the background were much like our high school band, playing in full force to support our voices and keep the energy moving. The Holy Spirit filled her house like the school spirit that permeated our ears, hearts, and souls throughout that packed gym. Mom taught me that day that when it comes to a spirit contest, you don't need a loud voice to win.

It was such a glorious day to see her rebound in that way. It was a gift not just for me, but for all of us, to experience the pure joy of having her back as both a mom and a proud Mimi. My mom was the star athlete of her own pep rally—front and center. And the crowd went wild.

Chapter 10

Clean the House — the Exterminator's Coming

"Wake up! The exterminator is here!" I opened my eyes to see Mom scurrying about, picking up the red and blue chips from my Connect Four game from the floor and pushing our dresser away from the wall.

"You girls, hurry and get up. Help me clean this stuff up and move everything out of the way!"

In Mom's world, everything truly meant *everything*—clothes and toys from the floor, furniture, and even our bed. In between her favorite curse words ("shit" and "damn"), she blurted out how she forgot to write "pest control" on the calendar, how messy our rooms were, and how we couldn't let the spray get on any our belongings. There was no time for me to whine back. There wasn't even any time to use the restroom. We were in a race against time as the pungent smell of pesticide made its way from the front of the house. It was a far cry from the bacon and eggs aroma that welcomed me most mornings. *This is so stupid. Why does she have to be so nitpicky? He's just the exterminator!*

Startled and afraid of Mom's unexpected morning wrath, my rapid heartbeat jolted me out of bed. Still dressed in my pink flannel nightgown with my tangled rat's nest hair in my face, I began moving things around with the speed and efficiency of a band roadie setting up a concert stage.

After the stress of that chaotic morning, Mom learned her lesson. From that point on, she made a habit of writing the words "PEST CONTROL" in bold red ink on our kitchen calendar. And fortunately, I never had to experience a helter skelter moment like that again—although I did suffer from an occasional bout of PTCD (Post-Traumatic Cleaning Disorder). The mere mention of cleaning my room could send my heart leaping out of my chest. To this day, I still break into a cold sweat at the memory of that frenzied early morning cleaning session.

Even back then, I knew that Mom's over-the-top reaction to the exterminator wasn't just about the possibility of toxic pesticides encroaching on our furniture and belongings. No, it had to do with her tendency to care about what others thought of our home (heaven forbid it was messy), which was in line with her perfectionist mindset about her appearance, her outlook on life, and her faith in God.

So … as soon as my siblings and I were old enough, Mom wasted no time putting her three healthy, capable, non-eager children to work. It became the norm for our cleaning crew to come together for occasions like birthday parties, family Christmas gatherings, and the occasional school or church meeting.

"Here," Mom would say, looking satisfied as she handed me a wad of Dad's old worn-out, white t-shirts-turned-rags and a can of Pledge furniture spray. "You get to dust the coffee table, TV, end tables, and all the picture frames."

Off I would go, totally sucked into Mom's reverse psychology. She had successfully convinced me that being in charge of cleaning the living room was a privilege rather than a chore. But it wasn't long before I caught on to her little tactic. If I dared complain, she'd say, "Just do it!"

Fortunately, the looming threat of her divine wrath was an equally strong motivator to get the job done right—or else! I was too scared of her sternly pointing out a rogue dust bunny and demanding that I "get back there and do it again."

Of course, it never failed that one of us would eventually cock an attitude while lugging the heavy dinosaur of a vacuum against the brown shag carpet. It was just a matter of time before one of us (usually Mom) would have to play mechanic and try to troubleshoot the burning rubber smell only to find nasty gunk stuck in the motor.

I never would have admitted this to Mom then (she would've assigned even more cleaning duties if she knew), but there was something satisfying about the smell of the Pine Sol that sealed our linoleum kitchen floor. I liked the way it felt to scrape off caked-on toothpaste from our bathroom countertops, and I liked the squeaky sound that could only be made by wiping a mirror with Windex and a sheet of newspaper.

When it was all done, I was rewarded with the awesome sight of a clutter-free living room with an end table vacant enough to rest our drinks and ample space on the floor to do an impromptu cartwheel (should the situation call for it). I'm almost positive that my uncanny appreciation for these simple pleasures was a stepping stone on the path to becoming the neat freak I am today.

I wish I could say that Mom's version of "Just do it" was as inspiring as a Nike commercial. Trying to keep my cool "or else" felt like a chore in itself as I stifled my huffs and puffs (and a few silent expletives) at the unfairness of having to upgrade our cleaning regimen for the exterminator. After all, he was just one person. Oddly enough, however, once he left, I felt the same satisfaction I felt when I cleaned for a party. It never failed—whatever Mom cared about, I ended up caring about, too. She would sigh a relieved "Ahhhh" as she sat there admiring the clean, spacious view from her cozy recliner.

"Now, doesn't this house look nice?" She would say while reaching for her plastic mug of diet soda resting on the dust-free, clutter-free end table.

Interrupting her bliss to showcase mine, I'd shout out, "Look, Mom. Watch me do a cartwheel!" Then, we'd both smile, sharing the same feeling that all was right with the world—all thanks to the simple pleasure of a clean house.

❧

When Mom miraculously came back to life right before our eyes that day before she passed, it was even more difficult to come to terms with her descent once her "rally" was over. She was fading more and more by the day, sometimes by the minute, and there wasn't a single thing we could do about it. While I tried to stay grounded in my faith and remember that God was in control, I couldn't help but buck His system every now and then. I often caught myself coming up with my own plan of how to make Mom's transition easier—not just for her sake, but also for the sake of my own sanity.

Besides praying, the only way I knew how to combat my anxiety was to keep myself busy. Somewhere in my DNA, the control freak gene took over, morphing me into a real-life version of Margaret Houlihan, the notorious nurse from the TV series, *M*A*S*H*. Administer morphine? Check. Rotate Mom's position in bed? Check. Make sure Mom is fresh and clean? Check. Apply a dab of her favorite lipstick? Check. Offer her tearful kisses, hugs, and mega-doses of love? Check.

One would think that skillfully accomplishing these duties would be sufficient to satisfy the soul of this sad, overthinking caregiver. But it wasn't. After obsessively tidying up Mom's room for the umpteenth time, making sure the oxygen tank was carefully positioned out of the way of visitors, cleaning up the residue from medication spilled on the bedside table, throwing away empty syringes and mouth swabs, folding washcloths, and rearranging toiletries for the next round of care, I finally broke down.

There, kneeling at the foot of her bed with nobody around but Mom and the gut-wrenching sounds of her ragged breaths, I cried out, "I don't know what else to do, Lord. Help me. I can't stand seeing her this way. I hate this."

Right then, I heard my brother come into the house and head toward the bedroom. I shot up, cleared my throat, and quickly wiped my face. Heaven forbid he would be able to see any evidence that the efficient, confident, and take-charge Margaret Houlihan had just lost it.

Knowing that Mom's end was near, I decided to spend the night at her house that evening in a last-ditch effort to buy as much time with her as I could. As I lay there in my old bedroom, I noticed that the only remnant from my childhood was the yellow paint on the walls (my favorite color since as far back as I can remember). She had transformed the room after I had moved out. First, it became a spare bedroom where her grandbabies slept during overnight visits. Then, once the grandkids grew too old for sleepovers, Mom converted the room to her own private sanctuary. It was a sitting room of sorts, where she meditated in her rocking chair next to an end table piled high with devotionals, prayer books, and of course, her rosary.

Staring at those yellow walls, I was overcome with nostalgia for the good old days. I wished I could travel back in time to my middle school and high school years, when my bedroom had been a safe haven that held the deepest secrets. It was where I boldly broke my parents' rules, drastically exceeding my allotted phone time and ending up on restriction whenever I got caught. And it was where I spent countless hours daydreaming about boys and gazing at my wall-to-wall posters of John Travolta and Lionel Richie. That room was a time capsule of memories for me, but the memory I longed for most of all was the feeling of being carefree with the future wide open … and no cancer in sight.

Tears from every stage of my life flooded onto my pillowcase, drenching the fabric and diffusing the comforting aroma of the Lozano Family Signature Fragrance: a non-perfumey scent with a touch of antiquity that always saturated the air and furniture. It must have been exhaustion, grief, or insanity that made me believe Mom would walk into my room right then and there, happy and healthy. She would gently plant a goodnight kiss on my cheek, teasing me that she would wake up me bright and early with one of her quirky and creative morning wake-up calls. I giggled and sobbed simultaneously, fumbling through my thoughts and wondering if it was time for another dose of Xanax.

With my heart and mind clogged with every emotion under the sun, I managed to entertain one more agonizing thought before drifting off to sleep. It was a flashback from earlier that day of my desperate prayer for help at the foot of Mom's bed, reminding me that I still had some worrying to do. *Oh, God, I need you. I don't know what else to do. Relieve me from this helpless feeling, and show me what I need to do so that Momma doesn't suffer.*

Lulling myself to sleep with my battle cry, I finally dozed off, only to be awakened six hours later by a soft and subtle whisper in my ear. *Clean the house; the exterminator is coming.*

Half asleep, I thought, *Wait a minute. Who said that? Am I dreaming?* I quickly opened my eyes, hoping that the early morning sunlight that was peeking its way through the window shade would shed some light on who was behind the mystery voice. Before I could begin to blame grief for what I thought might be a psychotic episode, I had this inner knowing—the kind that comes with goosebumps, suggesting that this unexpected, yet familiar expression was legit. Except this time, there were no

PTCD symptoms, no regressing back to my heart beating out of my chest, fearful and rushing around like a madman with a rat's nest for hair. I was completely at peace, knowing I had just heard from a divine source.

To this day, I still don't know if that neutral, loving voice belonged to God, my guardian angel, or my mom's spirit. All I knew at that time was that my prayer had just been answered. *If Mom cared how the house looked around family, friends, and* EVEN *the exterminator, surely she'd want the house to look nice and tidy for her heavenly guests, who were about to come get her.*

Lying there in bed, chuckling over the fact that I survived the dog days of childhood cleaning and PTCD, I thanked God for bringing forth such an iconic message to set in motion my next plan of care for Mom. It would be my last ditch effort to make Mom (and admittedly myself) even more comfortable as her hours on earth were winding down. I was just thankful for the role God had given me to play, no matter how small or simple it was.

As I stood in the kitchen, drinking a concoction of cream with a side of coffee and hoping my grief-stricken stomach could tolerate it, I scanned the house and my own mind for areas that needed cleaning. An accumulation of old and current mail, daily newspapers, shopping catalogs, and sugary snacks covered the kitchen table and counters—not to mention the clutter of photo albums and sixty-seven years' worth of pictures of Mom's history that had been set aside for the funeral services. A wave of claustrophobia, mixed with the realization that Mom would've had a cow seeing that mess, prompted me to alert the troops (a.k.a. as my siblings, Mark and Monica). Mom's original cleaning crew was about to be back in business.

I was sensitive to their somber demeanor and blood-shot eyes as they staggered their way into the kitchen that morning, so I contemplated how to gently tell them that their neat freak sister (a quality that used to get on their nerves) had a new idea. After all, the safety had been off on our trigger words for months, and I was in no mood to set them off. But my urge was too strong. Taking a deep breath, I blurted out, "You know what? I think we should clean up this house." Pointing toward the messy evidence, I added, "I mean, look at all this crap. You know Mom would be so embarrassed if she knew her guests saw this."

Surprisingly, they were quiet, slightly nodding their heads as they followed my pointed finger around our little pig sty (Mom's favorite term). Gun shy at the possibility that everything might be blown out of proportion, I decided to press the panic button, sharing with them the details of my midnight wake-up call. But by the time I got to the part about the heavenly guests coming over, I had lost it.

Maybe it was their sleepiness, guilt, empathy, or ability to recognize a divine message—but no war of words was exchanged. We were all on the same page, making sure that Mom's long desire of having a clean house was fulfilled.

As we headed toward the clutter, ready to take on our melancholic world with newfound purpose, Monica stopped in her tracks, turned to me, and sharply asked with a hint of teenage attitude, "We don't have to dust, do we?"

"No, just pick up," I chuckled, realizing that she was being both funny and serious at the same time.

Within a few hours, the floors were clear of our sprawled out luggage, and there was enough space on the dining room table to actually sit down and eat. Feeling excitement and a sense of relief at the success of our team effort and the fact that Mom's house was presentable to everyone—her physical family and friends, spiritual guests, and, yes, even the exterminator—I headed toward her room to release the cleaning energy I had left over.

Mom's breaths were slow and shallow. I quietly reorganized the bedside tables covered with a spiral note-book, medicine vials, packaged syringes, and toiletries. I even went so far as to rearrange the chairs in the room so that when each guest sat, they would have a clear view of Sleeping Beauty.

There was, however, one chair I put in the corner of the room, which was reserved for Mom's guardian angel. In Dr. John Lerma's book, *Into the Light*, he recounts a memorable story about one of his hospice patients. The woman would ask visitors not to sit in a particular chair in her room because she had seen her guardian angel sitting in it. In the midst of my emotional turmoil, I managed to find a tremendous amount of peace in that spiritual tidbit. Knowing Mom and her characteristic others-oriented mindset, I knew in my heart she would want her angel to be comfortable.

Later that morning, with tears in my eyes, I bent over to kiss Mom and whispered, "The house looks so good, Momma. It's ready. It's ready for Jesus, Mother Mary, Dad, Nana, Popo, and all your angels who are about to take you home. I hope this makes you happy."

Mom remained unresponsive. Still, I understood that on a soul level, she was aware of what was happening around her and was content knowing that her baby girl's prayer had been answered. Thanks to the simple, tried-and-true remedy of cleaning the house, all felt right in the world, even if only for the moment.

Chapter 11

You Are My Sunshine

From the time I started talking in complete sentences, my entire family had to refrain from pulling their eyeballs out every time I opened my mouth. Who could blame them? It took me what felt like forever to get my message across.

The start of my kindergarten year, my teacher confirmed that I was indeed a stutterer. It was so bad that some not-so-nice boy blurted out to me, "Hey, you talk just like Porky Pig! Th-th-that's all, folks!" He was right. My spirit animal had been identified, introducing me to a whole new level of insecurity, which caused more anxiety, making me sound even more like Porky Pig.

My teacher suggested speech therapy for me at school. Mom wasted no time in getting me a professional, someone who could be on her team in getting her little girl to slow down. In the meantime, Mom tried her best to help.

First, she coached me to slow down my words and take a breath between each sentence, but that didn't help. My dad tried to boost my confidence by making me watch TV shows featuring the famous country singer and stutterer, Mel Tillis.

"See? He doesn't stutter when he sings." Believe it or not, that wasn't helpful, either.

My impatient siblings rolled their eyes and interrupted my repetitive *Wh-wh-wh* sounds to loudly correct me: "What!" Or to my long, drawn out *A-a-a*, they would shout, "AND!" Surprise, surprise—that didn't help either. Not only did it make my stuttering worse, but it also brought out the mother bear instinct in Mom, who defended me with a stern, "Will you let her finish?!"

We all stood inside a vortex of tension while I carried on with my fragmented sentences. Just hearing Mom defend me in her Judge Judy style was enough to give me my power back during those moments when my vulnerability was at its peak.

Despite growing up with a mouth full of tangled and trapped words, I somehow managed to find the silver lining in my speech impediment, even comparing myself to the famous singer, Elton John. The first time I heard the song "Benny and the Jets" vibrating through the walls of my teenage brother's room, I felt relieved and even proud as the audience roared each time Elton sang, "B-B-B-Benny." It threw me into a new dimension of confidence.

Running into the kitchen with goosebumps traveling all the way into my throat, I cried out, "M-m-m Mom.

D-d-diiid you kn-kn-know El-El-Elton John s-s-s-stut-terred, t-t-too?"

She didn't even try to correct me. She just hugged me. "It sure sounds like it. Isn't that something?"

To this day, anytime I hear "Benny and the Jets," I remember that magical moment when validation beat out vulnerability and when I imagined Sir Elton John and Mom were secretly conspiring to help me feel normal.

Unfortunately, it wasn't just my stuttering that fueled my high-strung nature. If you asked my sister, she would roll her eyes and flat-out assert that I was a brat. What can I say? Back in the seventies and early eighties, terms like "separation anxiety" and "Attention Deficit Disorder" barely existed in medical journals and diagnostic manuals.

It all makes sense now. Before kindergarten, I was the child who screamed and cried as I was peeled away from Mom every time she dropped me off at the bowling alley nursery. I was her Tag-Along-Buzzard child, TAB for short—a title I proudly carry to this day. It was given to me by my dad and siblings, who watched with amusement (and sometimes annoyance) as I was Mom's little shadow. I never gave her a break. I would follow her around the house, even waiting outside the bathroom door until she was done. Once that stage passed, I graduated to "squirrel moments," always talking her ear off and rambling about off-the-wall topics. One moment, I would beg for permission to eat a snack before dinner, and the next, I'd pester her to buy me the latest and greatest toy on the shelf. I was more than just a handful; I was a mind-full.

Minute by minute, day by day, I witnessed my helter skelter-looking mom play whack-a-mole with my every irritating need, every stammering word, and every fragile emotion. Just when she was about to lose it, I'd hear the squishing sound of the cushioned seat as she retreated to her recliner.

"Come over here," she'd say, patting her legs. "Come sit on my lap."

In an instant, I'd quietly shuffle my pouty-lipped self toward her chair, knowing that what was about to come would be better than a verbal reprimand or even one of her quick swats on my behind. Mom must have realized how hypnotic those words were to me when she saw how quickly I decelerated from sixty to zero.

Without hesitation, she'd start to sing her sentimental favorite, "You are My Sunshine." Curled up close on her lap, I melted at the sound of her soothing voice while she patted my thigh with her right hand to the rhythm of the song and the rock of the recliner. Midway into the first verse, all my restlessness would come to a halt. Mom's, too.

Complete peace softened our space. Since I was plugged into Mom's heart from the time of conception, I always sensed there was more behind her go-to solution than chilling me out. Over time, my little subconscious mind revealed to me that I was on the right track. When I started to outgrow my stuttering, gain more self-control, and pacify myself, Mom found other ways to sneak in our special song.

I'm pretty sure the seeds of my sensitive nature, especially toward heartfelt songs, were planted during those occasional moments when I'd hear Mom's voice quiver during the verse: "You'll never know dear." *Pat.* "How much I love you." *Pat.* "Please don't take my sunshine away." *Pat.*

No matter how sick I was, she'd lie down with me with clear nasal passages from the secondhand fumes of Vicks VapoRub and softly sing my fever away. If I was watching TV, she'd get me out of my trance with a few pats on her lap, coaxing me to her. I'd go happily, one ear glued to the TV and the other glued to her chest. Within a matter of seconds, the vibration from Mom's voice and her heartbeat interrupted my daily scheduled programming. Life felt good.

This continued to some degree into my teenage years, and yes, even in my early twenties at times when I'd come home from nursing school and see Mom sitting in her recliner with a smirk on her face. Three pats on her lap was all it took to get me to join her. Up I'd go like the scene from the children's book, *I Love You Forever,* when the young boy became a man but still wanted to be rocked by his aging mom. I mimicked the scene to a T, practically crushing her lap. I still loved the time, attention, and rich history of our well-established love song.

I'm happy I didn't know then that our song would take on a different meaning years later. If I had, there would be no way in the world I would've understood or known how to handle it. But God in His infinite wisdom and timing had it all figured out, revealing to us how to share "You Are My Sunshine" one last time.

❧❀❧

How do I connect with my unresponsive dying mom? I asked myself. *How do I comfort both Mom and myself during this crucial time? How can I make a lasting impression on her heart that she can take back to heaven?*

Through the grace of God and an earth angel disguised as a hospice nurse, I found the answers.

The momentum was building as I witnessed Mom prepare herself for her heavenly getaway. I had just gotten accustomed to the new phase of seeing her mingle between both worlds, slipping in and out of deep sleep long enough to gain the energy for sweet and even profound waking times, where'd she track me with her all-knowing hazel eyes, open her mouth like a baby bird to take in her last drop of morphine, or receive a gentle swipe of a wet sponge swab to moisten her dry lips. Or when I was lucky, she'd respond with a nod or a frail whispered word.

Those rare moments became fewer and fewer as Mom fell into a deep coma, weaning herself from earth during her final three days with us. Another level of despair reared its ugly head. I struggled to catch my breath, knowing that the inevitable was coming and that all of our interactions—big, small, or mundane—were coming to a close. Many were gifts I didn't realize were gifts until the day they were taken away.

Frantic, I turned toward God, hoping for a quick fix to spare me from the black hole of grief that was about to suck me in.

Lord, please take her. This is too painful. I hate seeing her like this. I hate this!

God must have lost count of my repeated pleas over the course of Mom's illness, but this time was different. I needed a stronger dose of help. The anguish inside of me was so overwhelming that I secretly prayed the world would just end.

Come down and take us all right now. I don't care what you have to do. Just take us. I don't want to be a part of this life anymore. It's too damn hard. There's too much suffering.

To be clear, I wasn't truly suicidal. I could never leave loved ones behind in that way. It's just that I was so desperate to relieve the immense grief I was experiencing that I came up with this grandiose idea to escape from the pain and bring my entire family and close friends for the ride. Then, my imagination saw us all together, happy and whole in paradise.

Within minutes of my appeal for apocalyptic melt-down, God delivered the perfect dose of hope.

In the midst of waiting for the earth to tremble under my feet or the lights to go off, I was suddenly brought back to reality.

"Who is Papa?" the hospice nurse, Elizabeth, asked when I came back from a break. I must have looked confused, because she quickly added, "Your mom just opened her eyes and looked straight ahead, as if someone was standing in front of her, and called out to someone named Papa."

Through my nursing education, stories I'd read, and other deathbed experiences I'd heard about, including some of my own family and friends who had passed away, I'd learned that it's not uncommon for dying patients to see and even interact with their deceased family members right before they cross over. I've always found it fascinat-ing that God would allow such spiritual exchanges to take place to comfort not only the dying, but also those people at the bedside who were there to witness it.

Pumped up enough to ditch my grief aside for the moment, I excitedly asked, "Umm, are you sure she didn't say Popo? Her grandfather and father both went by that name."

But no, the nurse was adamant that she had heard "Papa."

"I'm positive. She leaned forward in bed and had the sweetest look on her face as she called out to him. When I asked her who she was seeing, her eyes began to close again, and she didn't respond."

In my mind, I flipped through images of Mom's family tree like a Rolodex, trying to figure out who this mysterious Papa was. But for the life of me, I couldn't. My brain was too clogged with grief, stress, and even a bit of jealousy that the nurse got to experience that phenomenal moment without me. I put the question aside, but it continued to linger in the back of my mind.

Later that day, Mom's sister, Barbara, stopped in for a visit. As soon as I saw her walk in, I made a beeline in her direction, hoping she could bring my mind's spinning Rolodex to a halt. I greeted her with a quick hug before giving her the rundown of Mom's close encounter of the heavenly kind.

"Was there a Papa in the family?" I asked, unable to contain the urgency in my voice.

Aunt Barbara nonchalantly replied, "Yes, 'Papa' was the name we called our great grandfather."

Somehow, another round of tears welled up from my soul's already depleted reservoir as I hugged my aunt, awestruck at Mom's surprise visitor. Half of those tears were solely for the realization that her divine meet-and-greet moment with her Papa meant one more thing: that God was giving me a heads-up. I knew Mom's departure time was imminent.

As much as I tried, though, I couldn't hold onto the relief of that awestruck feeling. My grief was just too overpowering. During the past week of Mom's hospice stay, I had told her repeatedly that it was okay to go and not to worry about us. But now that her Papa had come into the picture, I felt a sense of urgency to remind her one more time, just in case the morphine clouded her memory. Looking back, I may have been projecting my own insecurities onto her, and it may have been me more than anyone who needed to hear I was going to be okay.

Tearfully kissing every square inch of her face, I reassured her, "I see your welcoming committee is starting to come for ya, Momma." Between kisses, I added, "It's okay if you want to go. No more suffering, Momma. You hear me? No more suffering." *(more kisses)* "I'm going to miss you so, so, *so* much. But I'm going to be okay. We all are. I promise."

I closed by reciting her favorite quote that she used to say to us during our childhood and even to her grandchildren. I hoped she could feel every ounce of love that she had poured out to us: "I love you high *(kiss)* as the moon *(kiss)* and the stars *(kiss)* and the sun *(kiss)* and the sky."

It was then that I climbed into her bed and cuddled right next to her. The frailness of her body was overshadowed by her loud, shallow breaths. I desperately hoped she could feel my loving permission through the steady pulse of my heartbeat next to hers. Hoping she would respond with a movement or groan and wishing to rekindle our sweet bond just one more time—I got nothing back.

I started to sink into a deep pit of pain. No matter how hard I tried, I couldn't keep up with grief's sick game of tug of war. There was no winning. Small victories like tidying up the house for Mom's heavenly guests, surviving my many emotional breakdowns, helping family and friends get through their own mental anguish, making sure Mom was pain-free, giving her permission to leave this earth, and cuddling up next to her—they all fell short of the sustained peace and satisfaction that I desperately longed for.

Who was I trying to kid? Ever the overachiever and perfectionist, I couldn't grasp the fact that when it came to grief and caregiving, there was no such thing as sustained peace and satisfaction. Maybe periods of it, but nothing sustained.

As I slowly crawled out of bed, suffocated by the grief, God knew it was time for a booster dose of hope. Looking over at Elizabeth as she tended to Mom ever so gently, I thought to myself: *This is so depressing. How can she do this day in and day out?*

After reminding Elizabeth that I worked as a labor and delivery nurse, I confessed, "Man! I could never do what you do. It takes a special nurse to work in hospice. How do you do it?"

With infinite wisdom and compassion in her eyes, she replied, "Hospice is a lot like labor and delivery. You give a patient an epidural for pain. We give morphine. You coach the patients to breathe through a contraction. We coach the patients to take their last breath. You tell a patient to push. We tell a patient to go on to heaven. You see, we are both midwives of the souls, Marla. You can do this."

I started to sob uncontrollably. It felt as if she threw a rope down to me, rescuing me from my pit of grief with her words. And as I was climbing out, she added, "Oh, and always remember: anytime you are amongst the dying or in the presence of a birth, you are standing on holy ground."

Elizabeth's mindful words, coupled with my tears, totally washed away all the negative thoughts and emotions about grief that had accumulated over the course of eighteen months since my dad's passing. She spoke my language and gave me the dose of hope God intended for me; in fact, she may have given me an overdose. Thanks to her words, I was able to view those last two remaining days with Mom as sacred and beautiful. It fascinated me that my heart was capable of accommodating the extreme but contradictory feelings of both intense sadness and joy. Even though I was heartbroken to see Mom start to leave her physical body, I was happy knowing that I, as her Tag-Along-Buzzard-turned-spiritual-midwife, had the privilege of escorting her soul back to her heavenly home.

Later on in her shift, while Elizabeth was catching up with charting at Mom's bedside and I was tidying up for the gazillionth time, I surprised myself with a comical thought (a rare occurrence during that time). I wondered if part of Elizabeth's documentation included, "Talked patient's distraught daughter off the ledge. Daughter now calm and focused. Will continue to monitor progress."

Before I could smirk my way back to reality, Elizabeth inadvertently offered yet another dose from God's pharmacy of hope—just in case the last one had worn off.

"You know, I saw you talking to your mom earlier, telling her it was okay to go and everything. It was great you did that. I'm sure she heard your every word. Just remember to keep on talking to her, okay? Don't stop."

Divinely guided by her gentle reminder, I walked over toward Mom's bed, reflecting on the go-to strategy she once used to calm, comfort, and bond with her baby girl. Leaning forward, I tucked my left hand under Mom's, resting our intertwined fingers over her tummy as I examined her protruding veins and even pressed on them the same way I used to as a bored little girl in church. I marveled at the sight of her perfectly manicured hands and pink polished nails, which had somehow evaded the visible toll of the dying process.

As I held her hand in my own, my thumb instinctively began to stroke her skin to the tempo of our special song as I sang softly to myself: "You are my sunshine, my only sunshine. You make me happy when skies are grey."

It was then, mid-verse, when I felt something move in the bed. In slow motion, I watched in disbelief as Mom lifted the same right hand she'd used to pat me and moved it over to rest upon our clasped hands. *Oh, my God. Oh my God. Is this really happening? Momma hears me!*

Pausing for a split second to chuckle and cry over her impromptu response, I continued singing, this time a little louder, hoping the change in pitch would encourage her eyes to open. But it didn't, and surprisingly, I was okay with that. I was too enthralled over Mom's unexpected response to really care. Our hands felt as if they were connected in a flow of loving energy, similar to the feeling of our recliner days from my childhood.

Suddenly, afraid that our moment would come to an end with any kind of involuntary movement, I looked up and saw Elizabeth staring at us with her smiling eyes. Without making a sound, I mouthed the words, "Can you please go get my sister so she can take a picture of our hands?"

Within seconds, both of them rushed in. Monica's eyes were wider than mine as she quietly snapped away, capturing Mom's last form of communication.

As I savored our handholding moment a little longer, Elizabeth came over and sweetly patted my shoulder in confirmation. She whispered in my ear, "Every mother knows her child's voice."

Nodding, with a lump in my throat, I added, "Yes, and this one, right here, knows her child's heart."

It's hard to resist overthinking the various kinds of hell I put Mom through during the different stages of my life. I'm pretty sure her favorite go-to motto, "I swear, you're going to drive me to drink," started during the "You Are My Sunshine" years.

My bet is that if you were to ask Mom now about the secret to figuring out the perfect remedy for my emotional needs, she wouldn't just chalk it up to trial and error. Without hesitation, she'd boldly give God the credit, sharing the details of how His divine direction led her to pick out the right song for the right moment and even guided her to the right location, her recliner. She'd point out that at a soul level, we must've known back then to savor the special effects of the song and the memories that came with it, for it would one day serve as a catalyst for our hearts to reconnect one last time before she left her body.

How can I know Mom would say all that? Because this child, right here, knows her mother's heart.

Chapter 12

Lipstick—Never Leave Home Without It

*L*ipstick is magical to me. I'm sure its supernatural powers originated during my forty-week gestation inside the womb of the undisputable queen of lipstick, who valued lipstick almost as much as life itself.

Legend has it I experienced withdrawals after leaving the constant lipstick adrenaline drip from my mother's blood supply. By the time I hit five years old, I quickly developed my own fascination with the way it transformed not only her looks but even her mood.

Many lazy weekday mornings, after Mom had dropped off my siblings at school, I curled up on the couch with her, covered under a light blue wool blanket. I absorbed her melancholy mood as we watched her favorite soap opera, "Days of Our Lives." Often, I'd break away from her grown-up world to color or play with my toys while she vegged on the couch, resting from the demands of raising three kids under the age of ten.

But anytime I heard that deep masculine voice on TV say, "Like sands through the hourglass," I knew that an hour later, I would get to see Mom transform before my very eyes. I was always so excited to be part of her get-up-and-go routine. The whole energy in the house changed from that moment on. Like a little sergeant following her captain, I'd follow her as she opened the blinds to let the world know we were awake, tidy up the living room, change from our PJs, and march into her bathroom. I would either sit on top of the toilet seat or on the floor outside the open door, leaving her no room to think with my chatty patty-ness. Depending on what kind of mood she was in, she would either cheerfully chime in about "Sesame Street," my favorite toys, and other random subjects that popped into my little head, or she'd offer exasperated sighs and robotic "Uh-huhs."

Whatever her reaction, I'd sit there and study the wondrous way in which she put herself together. Intoxicated by the subtle floral scent of her favorite moisturizer, I'd watch her rub Oil of Olay on her flawless-looking face before dabbing and spreading her liquid foundation with the same bare fingertips (a practice that would make any modern makeup artist cringe). Then, I'd anxiously wait for her to swipe on some color, after which she'd dab and blow off the excess blush powder from a rinky-dink blush brush before gliding a frayed eyeshadow sponge over her eyelids with its caked-on shimmery taupe powder. By the time Mom's brows were filled in and eyelashes extended, her demeanor lit up as bright as her eyes.

A final quick pat with a puff of powder to her entire face meant that her makeup regimen was almost over and that it was time to have fun with my more awake mom. That was when the drum roll in my mind would begin. I'd sit on the edge of the toilet seat, leaning toward Mom in the same way she leaned into the mirror, and I'd mimic the funny faces she made as she perfectly coated her slender lips in a fluid motion with her favorite lipstick of the day.

Like clockwork, I'd hand her a sheet of tissue to blot her lips, and she'd chuckle at my surgical-grade precision as she pressed the tissue between her lips. Wanting to absorb every ounce of energy radiating from Mom's colored lips, I'd blurt out, "Kiss me, Mommy! Kiss me!"

Without fail, she would tightly pucker her lips and plant the most feather-light kiss onto mine, never once messing up her lipstick masterpiece in the process.

The world always looked more colorful after Mom applied her lipstick. At that age, I couldn't help but notice the correlation. If she felt good after glamming up, then I, too, was bound to carry out those same feel-good vibes for the rest of the day.

As the years went on, I graduated to Mom's mini personal assistant. I was frequently called upon to rummage through her purse in search of a tissue or an old envelope to blot her freshly coated lips. Sometimes, the job felt too much for me, trying to ransack through the black hole that was her purse while she rushed to get out of the house or drive her car. Mom had places to go and people to see. Heaven forbid she wouldn't look her best before stepping into the grocery store, post office, or a meeting with her fellow PTA moms. Once I managed to catch my breath, I would watch her routine with awe. It usually went something like this: apply, blot, and then ask, "There! How does it look?" She would clinch her pearly whites and add, "Do you see any lipstick on my teeth?"

Most of the time, she applied her current favorite shade perfectly. Occasionally, when I was at the top of my game, I'd spot a renegade dab of bright pink or red and wipe it away with one of my fun-sized fingers. Despite a few stressful moments, I loved my role as her lipstick inspector. It was a job I took very seriously, and I felt proud that she trusted me to help her look her very best.

My duties didn't stop there. At the tender age of five, I branched out into entrepreneurship, serving as Mom's personal massage therapist, mail and newspaper retriever, maid service, cuddle partner, and Tag-Along-Buzzard. But my favorite job of all was my recurring role as shopping buddy. Mom never failed to tip me for a job well done by splitting a candy bar or an apple fritter with me. It was the perfect treat that left both our hearts and tummies happy. Sometimes, she would voice regret over her choice of tips, seeing how she'd have to rein me in from the sugar's side effects.

There was one awful shopping trip, though, when my credentials were called into question, leaving me with no tip and a minor case of trauma. It happened at Globe, our local supermarket. In my little mind, it was the mothership of all stores. It was much like a seventies version of today's typical Wal-Mart minus the belt that rolls your grocery bags outside to your parked car.

Feeling excited as I usually did upon entering the automatic sliding doors, my emotions veered off into fear at the sound of Mom repeating her shopping gold standard: "Stay close by, so you don't get lost. You hear me?"

Nodding my head, I happily obeyed, knowing we had a good track record and that I'd always be safe and sound around her.

The store wasn't overly crowded, but that didn't stop me from holding on to her purse strap for dear life. My grip was so strong that by the time we reached aisle two, she told me, half-jokingly and half-annoyed, "Okay, you can let go now. My shoulder is starting to hurt." She grimaced and rotated her purse to the other side.

Taking her "stay close" instruction as literally as I could and without looking too obvious, I casually moved to that same side and grabbed on just as hard, adding more weight to her already loaded black hole of a purse. Looking back, I wonder if that anxious habit of mine may have been the primary culprit for the chiropractic adjustments Mom needed years down the road.

I was in the middle of the greeting card aisle, and Mom was browsing the top row, sifting through the plain, serious-looking cards. I felt safe enough to let go of her purse strap and started looking in the humor section. A few seconds later, I looked around and realized Mom was nowhere to be found. I panicked. Aisle by aisle, I scanned anxiously for a dark-haired lady carrying a tan purse with a long strap—a strap that I clearly shouldn't have let go of.

"M-M-Mommy?" I meekly cried out. *She's gone! She went home without me.* I was so convinced she had left the store that I bolted toward the front entrance to make sure our light blue station wagon was still parked out front.

Right then, a female employee who looked like a manager stopped me before the automatic doors opened. "Hey! You can't go outside. You need to pay for that!" I looked down and realized I was still holding a blouse that Mom had intended to buy.

"You need to stay here, little girl," she warned, taking the unpaid merchandise from my arms. Not only was I afraid, but now I thought I was in trouble. My panicky, yet timid cry became louder and out of control.

"I-I I c-c-cann't f-f-find m-m-myyy … umm … m-m-mmomyy!" I wailed.

Exacerbated by sheer terror, my chronic stutter was amplified by my sobbing, making my explanations that much harder for the employee to interpret. Her business-like demeanor scared me even more. Where was the compassion for this poor little lost girl?

She began walking me toward the customer service desk. After asking me some basic questions, she stood me next to a microphone that would have made Walter Cronkite proud, tapped it twice, and said, "We have a little lost girl by the name of Marla. She is wearing a light blue shirt and red shorts. Will her mother please pick her up at the customer service desk?"

No sooner had she cut off the mic that I turned and saw Mom rushing to the counter, looking scared, embarrassed, and stiff-lipped.

"Where did you go? I told you to stay by my side!" she scolded.

In between hugging her and wiping my tears and runny nose on her blouse, I stuttered, "I-I th-thought y-y-you left m-me and w-w-went h-h-home!"

Mom knelt down, held both of my arms, and looked into my tear-filled eyes. "I would never leave you," she firmly replied. "You hear me? Never! Don't ever think that, all right?"

Relieved and feeling safer than ever, I answered back with a long, drawn out, "O-o-o-k-k-kay."

From that moment on, I never believed again that she would leave me. Until thirty-six years later.

꧁♥꧂

As much as my heart felt like it was being shredded apart, I was ready—at least ready enough to follow through with our lipstick ritual one last time.

Knowing the time was near, I wanted Mom to look her best in preparation for meeting her heavenly ambassadors, who I'm sure were anxiously waiting to escort her back to her eternal home. I tried my best to tame my trembling hand as I lightly feathered her favorite shade onto her pale lips.

"Here ya go, Momma," I whispered. "You never know who you'll run into up there, right?"

She looked radiant dolled up in her L'Oreal Paris Mica #620 and her hair neatly brushed, while wearing her white flowy blouse to match heaven's color scheme.

On November 30, 2010, Mom's friend and night sitter awoke us at 3:45 a.m. after she noticed that Mom was starting to slip away. By the time we got to her bedside, she had taken her last breath and was in God's eternal home, undoubtedly welcomed by her personal fan club, including my dad, her parents, and other beloved family and friends. We had missed her transition by a few split seconds. She looked so peaceful. Just like Sleeping Beauty.

We cried over her, thanked her, hugged her, caressed her, and prayed over her. Without any effort, I embraced my anguish and the sacredness of that very moment simultaneously, not realizing that there was more to come.

After the hospice nurse prepared Mom for her transfer to the funeral home, my siblings and I were invited back into her bedroom. Mom looked radiant, but we noticed that she had a serene smile on her face—something that wasn't there before we left.

Immediately, I asked, "Did you do that?"

The nurse looked over at Mom with an expression of genuine surprise. "No, I didn't," she said. "I believe this is her own gift to ya'll."

The nurse was right. Leave it to Mom, the one who would go above and beyond when we were kids—leaving us notes in our lunch boxes and under our pillow before she went out of town—to give us one last miraculous parting gift to remember her by.

Comforted by her peaceful expression and knowing it was time for the funeral home workers to take her, I bent down to kiss her goodbye. It was then, when our lips touched, that I felt a small hint of her lipstick still on. Flashbacks from my "Kiss me, Mommy, kiss me!" days came rushing in. And for a split second, I felt the invigorating emotion of each one of those joyful moments. Gratitude set in, leaving me no choice but to thank God for those memories and the fact that Mom entered the gates of heaven whole, complete, and looking lovelier than ever—just the way she would've wanted.

Of course, I couldn't keep my emotional attention span set on any one dial. One minute, I was sobbing in deep grief. The next, I was smiling, strolling down memory lane, and thanking God. Then, almost reflexively, I was calm, rational, and in the zone, discussing final details with the hospice and funeral home workers.

As I sat beside Mom's lifeless body for the last time, I found my forty-one-year-old self regressing back to that panicky little lost girl at Globe Supermarket. I wanted to scream and cry out, "Mommy? Where is my Mommy? She's gone! She left me!"

It was then I heard a voice in my head. It wasn't the sound of the Globe employee who had once tried to help me find Mom. It was the calm, loving voice of God.

"I see you are lost, Marla. No need to be scared or to try to look for her. Your Mom is now with me. Don't worry. I will make sure she can still be with you, too—just in a different way. You won't have to search for her in fear as you once did. Because now her love remains with you and *in* you."

A renewed sense of peace hovered over me. I immediately snapped back into the adult version of myself, satisfied that the little girl in me would be okay after all. Filled with hope after my direct and divine reminder, which buffered my grief at least for the time being, I cried tears of relief as scenes of our reunion from decades earlier replayed in my head: *I would never leave you, you hear me?* I knew in my heart God was reassuring me that Mom would forever keep her promise.

From the moment of Mom's passing, I never looked at lipstick the same way. To me, it carries more magic now than ever before. Whenever I swipe my colorful magical wand over my naked lips, whether touching it up in the car or at work or as part of my morning routine, I can always count on feeling the sweet presence of my mom. As children, we can't know how a simple gesture or a lighthearted daily routine with our loved ones will later impact the rest of our lives—to the point that we end up using it to survive the grieving process.

Chapter 13

I'll Be Right Back

"*I'll be back.*"

I'd bet you ten dollars you read that in the Terminator's voice. But Arnold Schwarzenegger isn't the first person who pops into my mind when I hear those famous words. For me, the expression brings back an entirely different memory.

When I was a child, separation anxiety reared its ugly head every time Mom left my side (not just at the store). Of course, back in the seventies, there were no fancy dancy clinical terms to define what felt like sheer apocalyptic panic to me. It didn't matter whether we were at home or away. I'd drive Mom insane by taking my Tag-Along Buzzard role to the nth degree, sabotaging every one of her self-care attempts.

Starving for some me-time, Mom occasionally tried to break free from her little ball and chain, using the television or my siblings as a temporary babysitter. Before she knew it, my internal Mommy radar would sound the alarm, leaving her absolutely no time to read, talk on the phone, watch TV, water the plants, or even use the bathroom in privacy. Pure peace and quiet were rare commodities in her world. It was no wonder she usually seemed especially chipper right before she tucked me into bed—that is, if she weren't about to drop dead from exhaustion.

There was quite a long season between the ages of four and seven when it got so bad that just the sound from the other room of Mom's keys jingling could trigger my anxiety. Like Pavlov's dog, I'd reflexively dart toward the sound of her impending departure, ready to belt out, "Where are you going? Don't leave!"

By the time I could catch my breath, Mom would look exasperated and say, "I am *just* cleaning out my purse!"

Like a security blanket, her go-to phrase, "I'll be back," was a source of comfort for me, even though I didn't always show it. Over time, I learned that a slightly modified version—"I'll be *right* back"—meant she was maxed out, and I'd better listen. But I always clung to every word, whether spoken in patience or out of frustration.

Of course, if I freaked out over Mom's whereabouts in my own home, I most definitely took it on the road. When I was around preschool age, she joined an amateur bowling league. Each week before practice, she would drop me off at the bowling alley's nursery. I can remember hearing words like "clingy" and "Mommy's girl" floating around the stress-filled airwaves each time I was practically peeled away from her body as if I were never going to see her again. And I always ended up with one of my notorious nosebleeds. Needless to say, this would require Mom to come back to the nursery and help, inevitably resulting in another drop-off performance by yours truly. I can't imagine how frustrating it must have been for her to walk away from being in the zone with her bowling team so that she could tend to her baby girl.

Despite what felt like such traumatic moments during my early childhood, by the time I started kindergarten, I had learned to control my responses to unfamiliar situations. Such episodes had dwindled down to fleeting bouts of internalized anxiety, which I'm sure made it easier on not just Mom but everyone around me. I wish I could say the same for my one poor classmate, Billy.

His WWF performance of kicks, screams, and chair-throwing made my bowling alley scenes look mild—angelic even—by comparison. I was lucky because I had my mom's soothing words to serve as a shield from that kind of gut-wrenching meltdown.

"You're such a big girl. You're going to have so much fun today," she assured me on my first day of kindergarten. Trying to hold back tears that could've easily spiraled until I turned into Billy, I locked eyes with Mom as I gripped my shiny new aluminum Holly Hobby lunch box in a bold attempt to make her proud.

I'm sure she sensed my nervousness through my brave façade. "Remember, I'll be right back when school is over. Mommy will be waiting for you outside when you get out, okay?"

As usual, her words of reassurance, topped off with a gentle kiss and hug, were the perfect send-off. I nodded, feeling confident in her promise as I visualized all those times before when I was her official after-school pick-up buddy. I vividly recalled waiting for Mark and Monica to get out of school as we sat cooped up inside the family station wagon.

Looking back, I'm sure she did some serious praying in preparation for the Big K day. How else can I explain a no-tear, drama-free, and bloodless day of separation from the only world I had known for my entire life up to that point?

Each successful drop-off was a victory—not just for me but for Mom, who got to celebrate her own personal Independence Day over and over.

In my mind and maybe in hers, too, my big break-through at school meant the rest of my separation issues would magically disappear. But they didn't. I still couldn't shake the old habit of tuning into the sounds of metal jingling from her purse or the slow creak of the front screen door. If she did have to go somewhere, I did my best to taper down my reflexive freakouts, hiding my fear behind heart palpitations, stuttered questions, and faint whimpers.

Before I could evolve any further on the home front, my little nerves of steel were tested once again, setting me back to a whole new level of separation anxiety.

In July 1975, there was a highly publicized citywide search for a twenty-seven-year-old nurse who had been abducted from the same hospital where my uncle worked. For five days straight, all of San Antonio (my parents included) were glued to the TV and newspaper in terrified anticipation over this young, dark-haired, beautiful nurse's well-being. And there I was, the extra sensitive child with the Nosy Rosie ears (as Mom would sometimes call me) glued to my mother's fear. I eavesdropped on her somber conversations as she played private investigator with our family and her friends.

Five days after the nurse's abduction, news broke that she was found naked, bleeding from multiple stab wounds, and barely alive. Tragically, she died. The murderer had hidden in the back seat of her car before the attack. No matter where I was or what I was doing, I was consumed by the sadness and fear that jumped out from the front pages of the newspaper, the television screen, and the frantic conversations around me. How was an already anxious girl like me, who had just graduated to big girl status and who was trying to spare her mommy from her own worry, supposed to process this horrific story? Back then, there was no counselor to see and no how-to books on raising an anxious child who'd been traumatized. It was just me and my troubled mind, wondering if that murderer had an evil twin lurking around.

According to my six-year-old TAB brain, I had no doubt that Mom was next on his list to be taken away and killed. After all, she and the nurse bore some striking similarities—fair skin, long dark hair, and sweet smiles. I never actually mentioned any of this to my mother, of course. She seemed stressed enough as it was, and I didn't want to add to her angst by having her worry about me. So instead, I acted out, which I'm sure was just as bad.

In other words, I had to do everything in my power to protect her from being the next murder victim. Obeying my every racing thought before she left the house without me, I'd frantically remind her for the umpteenth time: "Don't forget to look in the back seat of your car, Momma. Okay? Make sure, nobody is there before you get in, okay?"

Depending on her mood or how fast she needed to leave, she would either respond with, "I'll be fine, dear heart," with a deep look into my eyes that temporarily knocked my panic level down from a ten to a five. Or she'd pause and clear her throat to ground herself from being thrown over the edge by my incessant requests. Then, she'd offer a curt, exasperated response and a quick hug.

Often, her go-to reply, whether rushed or not, wasn't sufficient for me. Sensing this, she would add, "Don't worry. I will check the back seat. Nothing is going to happen."

And off she'd go, only to find me at the front window moments later, spying on her to make sure she kept her promise. Nine times out of ten, I'd tap (or more likely pound) on the window to get her attention, pointing to the back seat just in case she forgot. My poor mom had to make an exaggerated move with her head, looking toward the back seat and proving to me that the coast was clear.

It seemed that once the hype of that awful news story died down, so did my fears—thank goodness. Lord knows I needed to get a grip because in just a few short years, another form of separation anxiety would manifest itself.

By the time I reached the fourth grade, Mom had climbed her way up the PTA ladder—so much so that her role as president required her to go to some out-of-town conventions for days at a time, leaving me behind with a less-than-warm-and-fuzzy dad and two teenaged siblings who lived in their own world. Armed and ready for what could potentially end up as the end of *my* world, Mom gave me the kind of heavy duty prepping that would've earned the approval of any modern day child therapist.

She broke the news to me after a fun bonding activity of baking her famous chocolate chip cookies together. As

I stood there in the kitchen, high on life and sugar (and still savoring the leftover cookie dough from the bowl), Mom gently dropped the bomb about her upcoming three-day departure.

"Hey, honey, I wanted to tell you that Mommy is going to have to go to an out-of-town PTA convention for a few days."

A few days?! I couldn't believe what I was hearing. Before I could search for my dusty old panic button, she beat me to the punch.

"Don't worry! I have everything lined up for these next three days. Aunt Barbara is going to take you to school and pick you up."

"Uh, huh." I nodded in approval. My aunt was like a second mom to me—kind, funny, and a lot less strict than Mom, so I knew I'd be okay in the nurturing department.

"Daddy or Monica will make supper every night." Mom really had all the bases covered.

As I sat there stewing in disapproving silence over her choice of chefs, she blurted out, "Oh, and here in a little while, you and I will go shopping so that we can find you something pretty to wear for picture day while I'm gone, okay?"

I perked up, knowing even at my young age that Mom's strategy of retail therapy was going to make me feel better. But then the reality of not seeing each other on picture day got to me.

Outwardly, I remained poised, trying to upgrade my big girl status, like pronto. But inwardly, I was already grieving her upcoming departure. Mom must have felt it, too.

"Don't worry," she said, showering me with hugs and kisses all over my face. "I'll call you every single night. I'll be back. It's only for three days."

Even though I was somewhat comforted by her thorough checklist and reassurances, my ten-year-old self couldn't fathom life without physically being near her mommy.

But I did it. And I'm proud to say that I did it well. Even though my original sadness lingered, I had several buffers in place. My dad did his best to be extra patient (which for him, was not an easy task), taking on the maternal role as he carried out Mom's instructions for me. There were loving notes from her hidden under my pillow and in my lunch box that he dutifully delivered. We even had decent meals to eat, considering that both Dad and Monica weren't very good cooks. The car pool trips with my aunt and cousins were the perfect distractions I needed to get by every day.

To top it all off, I got to wear my shiny new, aqua blue velour blouse on school picture day. I still remember feeling amazed by how cozy the fabric made me feel when I tried it on at the store.

"Every time you notice that nice feeling against your skin, that'll be like me hugging you. So smile pretty.

181

Okay?" Mom chimed in as I admired myself in the dressing room mirror. I carried out her loving instructions as the camera flash went off. Needless to say, that fourth grade portrait easily became one of my all-time favorites.

But the biggest and most effective buffer during our short season of separation had to have been Mom's hidden prayers. There's no other way to explain how I weathered such a sad, yet monumental moment of my childhood. As usual, her prayers and promises to always be right back remained powerful and true.

Thirty years later, those same prayers and promises from my childhood would be put to the test—whether I was ready or not.

⚜

My back was facing away from the rumbling sounds of wheels and bumps that kept getting louder as they rolled down the hallway of my childhood home.

With a quick scan, I took inventory of my siblings to make sure I wasn't alone in what felt like a nightmare. I noticed Mark standing near the front door, tired and somber-looking, while Monica lay on the couch in the back living room, asleep after a long and emotional night. And there I was in the middle, standing in the kitchen that had served as home base for Mom and her TAB for the past forty-one years. This was the home base where we never grew tired of eating her weekly Monday meal of pork chops, vermicelli, and beans. It was where we gobbled up her homemade chocolate chip cookies like scavengers, and where she accidently burned a turkey on Christmas of 1986, smoking up the house and setting off the fire alarm more than once. (Mom would say it was the oven's fault.)

But for me, home base was about so much more than food. It was a minor emergency clinic where she healed boo-boos with ointment, Band-Aids, and kisses. It was where I almost asphyxiated from vinegar fumes when she frantically tried to rid my hair of lice. Mom's patterned linoleum floor, scuff marks and all, was the perfect playground for me, my siblings, and even the grandkids. It was a space she could set up at a moment's notice for impromptu counseling sessions. It was where I vented and cried over long lost boyfriends, traumatic cheerleading woes, friend betrayals, and later on, nursing school stresses that triggered major anxiety. It was where we danced like nobody was watching and ram-rodded through every kind of homework assignment imaginable. As if that wasn't enough, the kitchen occasionally turned into a metaphorical boxing ring, where we'd swing emotional jabs at each other (I did most of the swinging), almost always leaving Mom the winner with a gentle but victorious swat to finish the match. And it was where we inevitably made up after every fight.

As I stood in the same spot, drenched in all those memories, I grappled with the idea of being present in the moment.

I can't look. I just can't ... but I need to. But I can't!

I heard the gurney wheels shift from the hallway carpet to the linoleum floor.

Oh, my God. Oh, my God! My entire body, even my tears, felt like lead, but I forced myself to turn and peek just a little. A blink's worth, to be exact. That was all I could take. I couldn't bear to see Mom leave her loving abode for the last time, shrouded in a maroon velvet cloth, and safely strapped on a gurney. I wanted to scream. I wanted to throw up. I wanted to die.

As soon as I heard the familiar sound of the screen door slam (the same sound that would've made me jump out of my skin a few decades before), my inner child came out in full force once again. I seriously thought God had it under control since He miraculously reassured us Little Lost Girls just a few hours before that Mom would never leave me. But grief isn't that easy.

Brave and a tad delirious, I headed toward the door. *Mommy?!?* I couldn't help myself. All the flashbacks of her saying, "I'll be right back," the rattle of her keys, the worn-out panic button inside my chest, the memory of her predictable loving (and sometimes impatient) responses—it was all too powerful to keep my inner child from total hysteria.

But by the time I made it outside and saw the funeral team carefully load Mom into the hearse, I snapped back to my adult self. It was a good thing because I don't think Mark could've handled another round of me losing it. He was so much like Dad in that regard. Dad hated to see us cry. Since Mark was just as fragile as I was, I didn't want to risk it. Plus, I wanted to be there for him, just in case he needed me.

I never even thought of going back inside to wake up Monica. Looking back, maybe it was a subconscious attempt to protect her from the pain of seeing Mom leave our house for the last time, or maybe it was just me being totally out of it, not thinking straight, consumed by my own emotions (probably some combination of the two). Whatever the case, I still battle with the regret of not waking Monica up to experience that moment with us.

Approximately three hours after Mom's passing, Mark and I stood there, arm-in-arm and controlling our tears as we watched the hearse drive her up the street and straight into the morning sunrise. I followed that precious cargo until my eyes became blinded by the sun's rays. It felt like a scene from a movie, and it was as beautiful as it was sad. So beautiful that I made a vow to myself to never forget the gift God had given to me in Mom's majestic-looking departure.

Fall also made itself known that morning. The chill in the air was just enough to pierce through my two-week-old jammie set that consisted of a mismatched old sweatshirt and paper-thin hospital scrub bottoms that I'd "borrowed" from work. Trembling from the temperature, as well as the grief, Mark must've sensed that he was about to see his baby sister break down. Without hesitation, he quickly channeled Dad's familiar old pattern and guided me up the sidewalk with his protective hold on my lower back.

"Come on," he sternly said with a sigh. "Let's get back inside."

The short walk felt miles long as I realized with each step that my Home Sweet Home no longer existed. I went inside, headed straight for my old bedroom, took a Xanax and went to sleep.

I could barely pray for almost a year after Mom's passing because I was so paralyzed with grief. I had to rely on the hope of other people's prayers to counteract my unintentionally half-assed prayers, which I felt were getting me nowhere.

Thankfully, God understood my little hiatus from Him that was now taken over by every stage of grief in the book. Shock, isolation, anger, depression, and acceptance all invaded my life. And I hated every moment of it.

My only saving grace was the memory of God's Little Lost Girl moment and the true blue belief that our loved ones show us their presence through heavenly signs. The problem was that I demanded proof of that ... almost every minute of my life.

From the time my Xanax wore off that day she passed, I became obsessed with keeping an eye out for a heavenly sign from Mom. What was a TAB like me, with a history of always looking for her mommy, supposed to do? If I wasn't searching, I was asking. If I wasn't asking, I was begging, either her or God, to show me something. *Show me a red bird. Please, Mom, come to me in my dreams. I want to feel you with me.*

I remember confessing to Monica how much I was seeking out the quick relief of a heavenly sign—or else.

"Man, Marla!" she blurted out in a way that only an annoyed big sister would. "Will you leave her alone? Just let Mom rest in peace."

Immediately, the mommy's girl in me lashed back. "She *is* resting in peace. I'm just asking her to show me, that's all."

I couldn't help myself. Grief made me do it. It was grief that made me doubt whether Mom would be right back, spiritually or otherwise. Despite my uncertainty over our new relationship, I managed to trust that God was going to take care of the details. And he did—more than a TAB could ever ask for. Just as Mom had promised—she came right back.

Chapter 14

Heavenly Signs

"See a penny, pick it up. All day long, you'll have good luck."

That line from *Grease* has basically been part of my DNA since age nine, when I first saw the film. I loved it so much that I must've watched it about a hundred times before my tenth birthday. Luckily for me, Mom was completely accepting of my *Grease* obsession and would watch with amusement anytime I belted out, "Tell me about it, Stud," or recite random trivia from the movie. (Looking back, I'm amazed by how much of the content should have only been intended for mature audiences.) Mom obviously recognized that her innocent baby girl had no clue that those heavy duty makeout scenes and bun-in-the-oven one-liners had anything to do with Rizzo yelling out, "I'm not pregnant!" at the school carnival.

Mom didn't need *Grease*, however, to turn her into the official Penny Picker-Upper. No matter where she was, what she was doing, who she was with, or how tight her schedule, she could always spot Abraham Lincoln's copper face from a mile away.

"Hold on, Marla, let me get this penny right here."

She'd quickly bend over to pick it up and then dance a little jig in celebration. I, on the other hand, would go into full-blown *Grease* mode. At the end of our ritual, we always flashed a subtle smirk or even a quick giggle at one another, content in our quirky ways. All the pennies Mom found were either thrown into her purse or tucked into her shoe until we got home, where she haphazardly tossed them on top of our refrigerator, ready to pay for school lunches or last-minute ice cream treats.

After her beloved father passed away in 1997, though, Mom's penny collection began to take on a more spiritual significance.

At that point, when I was a twenty-six-year-old, sleep-deprived, funked-out, postpartum mom, she taught me that a penny is a sign that our loved ones in heaven are always with us. I never questioned her, believing with my whole heart and soul that this kind of thing was real. I cherished the comfort it brought me as I tried to balance the sadness of losing my Popo with the joy of holding a new life in my arms.

Even Mom's whimsical reaction to finding coins started to change. Each time she spotted another penny, her face took on a noticeable softness. With much intent, she'd look up toward the sky, kiss the penny, and say, "Hello, Daddy," before carefully tucking her heavenly treasure into her leather coin purse or placing it inside her tennis shoe until she arrived home. But no longer did she store change on top of the dusty fridge. Now, her mission was to fill up her grandchildren's piggy banks with all of her daddy's heavenly hellos, along with any extra income God had blessed her with throughout the week.

When I witnessed this shift for the first time, I was so taken aback by the change in her demeanor that I forgot to perform my trademark *Grease* routine. Our quirky ways were over, and that was okay with us. We had graduated to a higher level of understanding, and we embraced it.

As the years went by, so did the passing of my Nana and my paternal grandfather. Mom was a devoted caretaker to both of them and stood by them to the very end of their illnesses. On top of my own grief at the loss of my last set of grandparents, I inherited Mom's sadness as I waited in dreadful anticipation to see how she would handle it all.

During the course of her grief journey, I watched in awe as her spirits rebounded—not just with finding pennies, but in other ways, too.

Before it was time to put Nana's and Popo's house up for sale, Mom routinely checked on the house and sat on their back porch swing. Their yard had served as the best stomping ground for Easter egg hunts, birthday gatherings, and lazy afternoon visits. To me, their well-groomed lawn always reminded me of a park, with its shady Arizona ash trees, cemented birdbaths, homemade bird houses, and colorful lawn ornaments.

I always knew that Mom's part-time duty was more like a kind of therapy for her. Often, on the days I would visit her, we would go to their house together, check on the mail, water the plants and the grass, and eventually end up on the back porch.

With each sway of the swing, I felt more and more helpless as Mom shared her tears, memories (both good and bad), fears about selling the house, and worries about how she was going to move on without them. The only way I could shield myself from breaking down along with her was to keep my breath in tempo with the creaky sound of the swing or with the melody of the nearby wind chime.

I will never forget the first of many instances when God interrupted the flow of Mom's litany of woes there on that back porch.

"Look over there. You see them?"

Recognizing the tiptoe tone in Mom's voice, I carefully glanced over and followed her gaze toward the brightly colored red birds perched firmly on a tree branch, chirping away as if to get our full attention.

"Isn't that something? Here we are talking about Nana and Popo, and they show up."

For minutes at a time, I sat there covered in goose-bumps, feeling as if we and those cardinals were the only living creatures on earth.

With a lump in her throat, she greeted them as if her parents were actually standing there in physical form. "Hi, Momma. Hi, Daddy."

Never once did I think she was crazy. How could I? The peace that came over her every time she saw a cardinal was sudden and palpable. This well-known heavenly sign had become popular from the time my Popo died, so much so that Nana and Mom's sisters received their red bird signs, too. Year after year, I watched them celebrate this connection by exchanging red bird ornaments during Christmas time and red bird yard decor in the spring, even giving each other red bird pajamas on one occasion.

Never in my mind or heart did I think that those penny or red bird signs were a bunch of BS. I didn't just believe because of my Mom's and other families' testimonies. I had my own encounters to conclude for myself that what I was being taught was indeed real.

I experienced a string of events in which every time I thought of my grandparents, I, too, was visited by a few red cardinals or saw a shiny penny.

My Heavenly Signs 101 class didn't end there. Before long, Mom kept telling me about how she would spot her parents' lookalikes in stores. It would take her breath away and make her question her last 20/20 vision exam.

There was one incident after Mom's mastectomy when the two of us both questioned our last eye exam. We were in her hospital room and both witnessed a heavenly sign together. The thermostat had gone out of whack in her room. The nurses and I kept trying to fumble with the dial to no avail.

It was getting late, and visiting hours were almost over. Mom's pain meds hadn't kicked in, and it was getting "hotter than hell" (her words, not mine). There was no way I could leave her in that state. Worried and feeling out of control, I silently prayed, asking God to fix this little setback—like, *stat*.

Right before I charged toward the nurses' station to request another room, we heard a knock on the door. "Maintenance. Can I come in?"

Eager and desperate, we welcomed the male voice inside, only to see a small metal ladder come through the door first.

With a softness to his voice, he poked his head around the ladder and aimed his smiling eyes directly at Mom "Hello, ma'am. My name is Ed. I'm here to fix your AC."

In that split second, a feeling of fresh air filled the room as if the AC had just turned on all by itself. But it hadn't. Mom and I looked at each other, and we just knew. We knew that there was more to this maintenance man than a quick repair. He was a gift from God. Mom started to cry.

"Sir, you look just like my daddy."

Ed appeared to be in his early seventies, had the same posture, the same hairline, the same full lips, the same beam through his slitted eyes, and really the same everything as my grandfather. He even had on the same style of Dickies work pants that Popo used to wear while doing chores around the house.

Thank goodness, the maintenance man was receptive to Mom's heavenly theory. He even stated that he himself believed in that, too, and gushed at how honored he was to be her daddy's doppelganger. He chuckled when he told us that he was supposed to get off work earlier but decided to stay for an extra hour to help out. Without prompting one another, we all agreed that Ed's overtime schedule was no coincidence.

By the time Ed left the room, all was well in our world. The AC was back on, Mom's pain meds had kicked in, and I was relieved, knowing I didn't have to go all out at the nurses' station like Shirley MacLaine in the movie *Terms of Endearment*.

"I hope you feel better soon," Ed kindly whispered as he swooped in, moving his oversized tool belt out of the way to give her a hug. "I will pray for you. Don't you worry. Everything is going to be okay."

What kind of maintenance man does that? I wondered, shaking my head in disbelief. I thought, *Only Mom*. She had always been a magnet for love and special encounters with complete strangers. The weird thing was that even though Ed was a complete stranger, he certainly didn't feel like one. At all!

"Thank you," Mom softly cried.

In the middle of their heartfelt exchange, my own heart sank at the sight of Mom's limited range of arm motion, which prevented Ed from receiving the gentle, yet full force hug that she was known for and that he so deserved.

All she could offer him was a few pats to his forearms, which about killed me inside. I hated seeing her suffer. And I could tell through her slight grimace that she wanted to give him more of her love.

Just about the time when *damn you, cancer* was about to make its guest appearance in my headspace, Ed started to say goodbye. I got up and hugged him with the full intention that my embrace was from Mom, too.

Both of us escorted Ed out the door with our words of thankfulness. Once he left, I turned around and saw how much my mother was moved. I made a beeline back to her bed.

"I feel like I just had a visit from Daddy."

I kissed each tear that streamed down her face, mixing hers with mine. "I believe you did too, Mom," I reassured her.

And for the next ten to fifteen minutes, before her pain meds induced her into La La Land, we rehashed every detail of Ed's visit with pure giddiness, from his looks and gestures to his words and his wardrobe, savoring our spiritual high.

"Quick!" Mom interjected. "Go write this down in the gratitude journal before we forget."

Even though I knew good and well that we would never forget, I did as I was told. After all, this was the kind of heavenly sign that was well worth recording.

And just like that, from her hospital bed, Mom indirectly taught me again how to recognize a heavenly sign when I see one.

During the years that followed, whenever Mom would get down about missing Popo, all I had to say was, " Hey, remember Ed?" and like magic, her pain was buffered. She would light up as we recalled the details of when she first met her earth angel.

As time sadly marched on with the passing of more of Mom's family members and friends, I never grew tired of listening to each story or lesson of how they all connected with her.

Often, she'd say, "You'll never guess what my dream was about last night" or "Guess what happened to me today" or "You know what's something?" My soul always knew what she meant. My soul knew to savor every mystical, supernatural, very real, and even woo-woo-sounding detail of what she was about to say. I knew I was going to be hit with another lesson about how our souls continue to live on from across the veil.

I seriously think Mom had no clue (and neither did I) that all of her past experiences with the pennies, red birds, lookalikes, and dream visits would be my Heavenly 101 class. It just fell in line with every other life lesson thrown at me throughout my lifetime. Mom and God knew I needed to pass that course. I'm sure if they were handing out grades, I would've gotten a big fat A+. There isn't a doubt in my mind that both of them felt it was necessary for me to pass that course in order to proceed to the next one—a course I definitely didn't want to take.

My Heavenly 102 class was waiting in the wings, so to speak, ready to give me my very own custom-made heavenly material handed out by my beloved Mom. Her promise of never leaving me was about to reveal itself. Was I going to pass this course? You bet I was. As much as it pained me to even have to be enrolled in this class, I was ready to score high with flying colors.

I was desperate.

The very next day after Mom passed, I waited for the doors of heaven to open, ready to welcome her. For some reason, I had expected to feel an instant sense of relief. I was certain that if Mom would intuitively come to the rescue for her TAB when she was alive on earth, then surely she would be on top of her game and do the same, if not more, from heaven. But reality failed to live up to my expectations.

For days after that, I got nothing. No red birds. No dreams. No sense that she was near. Not even a lucky penny. Nada! Feeling lost and confused and suffocating in my own sorrow, I walked around like a grieving lunatic from the time I woke up to the time I went to bed, constantly pleading and begging. *Please, Mom, show me a sign you're with me. I need you. I miss you. Please!*

I even got God involved. *Come on, God. Can you please allow her to give me a sign?*

Throughout my lifetime, Mom had instilled in me an instinct to always trust and believe in God's perfect timing on anything and everything, no matter what. In the back of my mind, I knew our moment of reconnection would come. But at that time, it wasn't coming fast enough for me.

A few days before her funeral, I went shopping alone for a dress. Since retail therapy was our favorite mother/daughter pastime, I thought I'd invite her to spiritually join in my shopping spree (just in case she hadn't received the memo that I needed not only her presence but her opinion to pick out the perfect outfit). *Oh, Mom. You always knew what looked best on me. Please be with me and guide me to the right dress for your funeral.*

In the same department stores where we used to shop, I stood in front of each three-way fitting room mirror, begging God and Mom to show me a reflection of what might have been—Mom standing behind me with her arms crossed, inspecting every detail of every outfit with either her you've-got-to-get-it smile or her no-way-in-hell frown. But I got nothing.

Time was running out. Defeated, crushed, and a little pissed off that my personal wardrobe assistant had abandoned me, I stood there in the fitting room and cried as I heard the manager announce that it was the last call for purchases before the store closed. This was my last opportunity to shop before the funeral. I didn't know what to do.

Clouded by my pain and a whole lot of misjudgment, I ended up buying the no-way-in-hell outfit. Even today, when I look back on the funeral, I wonder what I was thinking. I got a few disapproving head-to-toe glares at my short black skirt and lower-cut-than-it-needed-to-be blouse. As the years have gone by, each time I've been tempted to beat myself up again over my fashion mishap, I've jokingly turned it back to Mom. *It's all your fault. If you'd been there and shown me a sign like I'd asked, I would've picked out something better—but nooooo!*

Although it felt like an eternity—two weeks after the funeral, to be exact—I finally started to feel as if Mom was trying to make her presence known.

It started off with roses. Our pastime during the course of her cancer journey had been to notice and jot down every encounter with roses as confirmation that our prayers were being answered by God and through the prayers of Mother Mary and St. Theresa. So it didn't surprise me one bit that Mom chose the rose route to connect with me.

The first time it happened, I was shopping (of course) and stuck in my usual funk of missing her. While walking in the middle of a traffic-free aisle at Dillard's, I interrupted my regularly scheduled program of grief in my head and remembered that I needed to get something from the men's department. I must've been walking around like I was drunk because I made a sudden sharp turn and was jabbed in the arm by a metal hanging rack sticking out from the lingerie aisle.

Before I could belt out my go-to cuss word at the startling pain shooting down my arm, I looked up and was hushed by the sight of a cute black blouse covered in a massive amount of bright red and pink roses.

I stood there in shock, rubbing my arm as I tried to process how I got from Point A to this heavenly feeling Point B. My mind was spinning, yet my heart remained grounded. I touched the blouse. I felt Mom. I inspected every rose embroidered on the fabric. I felt Mom. I noticed there was nothing else on the rack but that one blouse, which was obviously in the wrong department. And I felt Mom.

Within seconds, the floodgates burst, and every emotion came spewing out—joy and pain, relief and awe. *I love you, Momma. I know you're here.* Sigh.

Oh, Momma. Double sigh.

It was my first heavenly sign, and it was in public. There I was struggling not to look like a psycho as I tried to suppress my overactive tears, my somewhat loud one-sided dialogue, and a strong compulsion to bury my head inside this divine piece of merchandise.

With my spirit renewed, I walked away from the scene, having no clue that this stint with roses was going to be "our thing" for quite some time.

From then on, it never failed that anytime I thought of Mom, I'd soon thereafter come in contact with a saleslady, a patient at work, a bank teller, or even a complete stranger named Rose, Rosie, Rosa, or Rosemary. Or I'd come across a Facebook post, book, magazine, or even a billboard sign that somehow incorporated an image of a rose. Anytime Mom popped into my head, I saw a rose.

I cherished each rose sign, big or small, and used each one as a sweet Band-Aid to mend my broken heart. Of all the signs Mom graciously gave to me, there were two major ones that I like to call "Big Kahuna Signs." They tipped the scales in the heavenly floral department.

The first of these happened about a month after her funeral. Out of the five roses I had hand-picked from the top of her casket that dreadful day, I noticed two remained in full bloom. One was bigger than the other, symbolizing to me a mother with her baby—Mom and me.

Energized by my God wink, I immediately called our old neighborhood florist, Mr. Gembler, to ask if he had sprayed some kind of preservative on Mom's floral arrangement. He denied using anything of the sort, stating that all his roses are fresh and usually last about a week.

By the end of our conversation, we both agreed that I had a special blessing from God sitting on top of my kitchen counter. How could these roses have lasted an entire four weeks? I was in complete awe.

Once again, I felt Mom. And once again, I broke down—but in a good way. Now that Mom's spirit was becoming more easily recognizable, especially in this Big Kahuna kind of way, my feelings of grief and loss were replaced by joy in our newfound spiritual connection.

As if that heavenly sign wasn't enough, Mom and God teamed up for a second round of rose-filled wonders. This time, it was meant to soothe not only me but also those other family members who loved and missed her just as much as I did.

It had only been six months since her passing when my brother, Mark, Mom's firstborn pride and joy and her only son, was to marry at the tender age of forty-eight. He had found his perfect match, Priscilla, a few years prior, when Mom and Dad were both still alive, and they had loved his bride-to-be. Mom had been so excited about her upcoming role as mother of the groom that she picked out her dress the moment the news broke in sweet anticipation of the big day.

It seemed that no matter how loud the joyful wedding bells rang around me in the weeks and days before the ceremony, there persisted a low vibrational background tone of pure pain that kept trying to drown out the happiness. I kept being reminded that my beloved parents were going to be no-shows. *On the other hand, I knew better.*

Prepping my heart for this monumental day, I made a formal invitation in deep faith, asking and even begging Mom to show me an obvious sign during the wedding that she and my dad were there with us. *Make it big, Mom. Make it obvious. I know how much this wedding means to ya'll. Come and show that you and Dad are celebrating with us. Please.*

As hard as it was, I tuned into the beautiful ceremony with the full intention that any tears I shed would be exclusively reserved for the joys of matrimony. But as you can guess, it didn't work out that way. My mind couldn't get past the excruciating thought that my parents were not physically present to celebrate with us.

After the wedding ended and the bridal party made their way back to the altar for pictures, we all headed toward the church foyer. Walking arm-in-arm with one another, I could tell that every single one of us was riding the same bittersweet wave of emotion.

Somehow, grief had turned up the volume of my pitiful background music loud enough for everyone to hear.

But just as I was about to lose it, the strong aroma of roses filled the foyer.

At first I thought, *Man! Someone is wearing some heavy duty cologne.*

I started to sniff the people around me like a bloodhound, including the necks of my very tall teenage nephews, who looked at me like I was nutso. Nothing.

I scanned the room, thinking I'd either see one of the bridesmaids holding her bouquet or maybe a big floral arrangement displayed nearby. Still nothing.

By then, the scent had become so strong that I felt like I had just stepped into a floral shop filled with roses from wall to wall.

Then, it finally hit me. *Oh, my God, this is it. The sign! The sign!* I felt Mom. I felt the power of her spirit converge with the sweet fragrance circulating around me—and to top it off, she brought along Dad. His fatherly presence was just as palpable, and for a brief moment, I didn't feel like a grieving orphan. My soul was vibrating at such a high level that I practically felt myself floating toward Monica.

"Do you smell …?"

Before I could finish my sentence, my fellow-believer-in-heavenly-signs sister sniffed and blurted out in awe, "Yes! Roses!"

Holding back tears, we scanned the foyer from top to bottom with our noses leading us straight toward heaven. I wanted to yell for all to hear, but I remained quiet.

Oh, Momma and Daddy, I love ya'll so much. Thank you for coming. Thank you.

Within seconds, a few family members had gathered around us and caught on to my parents' surprise visit. Not one of them could deny the link between the story of my parents' formal invitation and their aromatic arrival.

To be able to experience this kind of Big Kahuna sign with others validated not only that heavenly signs are for real, but that I'm not crazy.

Since then, Mom has continued to make her presence known in so many ways. She continues to follow her parents' tradition of shining her spirit through the numerous red birds that fly my way, always at just the right time. Sometimes, when a red bird lands near me, I talk as if Mom is standing right there—the same way she did with her parents.

Often, when I talk out loud to Mom, more signs tend to follow, as if she's answering me. For instance, once during a fragile moment when I thought I was the World's Worst Mom, I went on a walk to try to shake off the doubt that plagued me. Remembering the brat that I was while growing up, I began to think of how my mother must have also felt during her fragile times. I called out to her: *Thank you, Mom, for loving me even when I acted unlovable.*

Shortly after I cried out to her, I looked down and saw a penny on the ground. Of course, I immediately thought of Mom. When I picked it up, I saw that the date etched on the face of the coin was 1969—the year I was born.

What were the chances of finding a forty-eight-year-old penny in my neck of the woods precisely at a time when I needed it most?

I kissed my special penny and held it close to my heart, crying as I swayed to the rhythm of my quiet words of praise and thanksgiving.

Thank you, God. I love you, Mom. I love you, Lord. Thank you, Mom.

I truly felt that was her way of telling me that she was listening and to reassure me that I was going to be okay as a mother. And thanks to her and God teaming up in that miraculous way, I was.

I have basked in the glory of so many of her heavenly signs, but none has impacted me more than her dream visits. On several occasions, these encounters have jolted me awake with overwhelming sensations of sensory overload, knowing that I had just seen Mom in living color, looking healthy, vibrant, and peaceful.

Each time, I've awakened and realized that it wasn't really a dream. God knows me well. He knows that if Mom ever appeared to me in physical form (like I've asked at times), I'd most likely faint from the overwhelm. So He's kind enough to allow Mom to connect with her baby girl through dreams. My usual whacked-out sequence of emotions is a dead giveaway to the realness of it all. I cry tears of pure euphoria over the fact that I was just gifted with looking into her eyes, touching her through a deep hug, and hearing her voice, whether audible or telepathic. While my heart keeps its hand on the save button for as long as possible, my mind eventually takes over, bringing me back to the state of missing her all over again. Then, I cry like I did on the day she died.

It's been almost ten years, and I still react the same way to those Big Kahuna dreams. They may wreak some minor emotional havoc, but I wouldn't have it any other way. For one, I get a glimpse of Mom in all her heavenly glory. But on top of that, I'm blessed with the divine understanding that this is all part of my healing journey, designed especially for a TAB like me. And for that, I am grateful.

I'm proud to say that even though I've already made the honor roll in my new Heavenly 102 class, I'll never stop working to further my education in this most important, life-changing gift from God.

If ever you doubt whether you are a candidate for blessings like these, let me reassure you that you will—I repeat: you WILL—experience these special encounters with your beloved. Be ready. Be open, dear Earth Angels, and have faith that through God's grace, He will provide you with perfectly timed heavenly signs to prove that our loved ones are with us for eternity. You never know where you might find one, whether a penny, a bird, the scent of roses, or even a tube of lipstick. Just know that your Heavenly class will forever be in session.

Acknowledgments

To my very first editor and beautiful niece, Allison Pope: if it weren't for you saying yes to taking on this project with me four years ago, I'd still be a mess and stuck on chapter one. Thank you for sharing your gift of writing and editing with me and for easing my mind through it all. You made me become a better writer in so many ways. Even through your pregnancy, breastfeeding, raising a toddler, and everything in between, you managed to keep me on track with my blogs, my book proposal (that was a doozy), my social media content, and this book with your impeccable editing skills. I will be forever grateful for the sweet exchange we shared, between your editing and my taking care of sweet baby Adrian (a.k.a. Chulito). It was all such a blessing. I'm so proud of you, sweetheart.

Special thanks to my editor, Melanie Votaw for helping me put the final pieces of my book together and for appreciating my story. God knew I needed your keen eye, expertise, kind heart, and professionalism, as well as your gentle and motivational spirit to bring this part of my life's purpose to fruition. You will always have a special place in my heart for all you did for me.

To Sabrina Stolle, my best friend since kindergarten: there are not enough words to describe how truly grateful I am for the way you walked me through yet another big season of my life. Whenever I felt like pressing the panic button or sending out a praise report during this book journey, you, like always, were at the top of my list to call. I will forever appreciate your honest and sound advice and your intuitive way of soothing my soul with your God-given gifts. You are the best buddy a girl can ask for. LYLARS—always and forever.

Special thanks to my best friend since middle school, Kelly Howell. Your calming effect has always been your superpower. From the time you held my hand as I nervously spewed out all those Hail Marys during cheerleader tryouts to now with this book journey, your patience and support have forever remained. Thank you for never changing and for being the beautiful soul sister that you are.

A loving shout-out to Martha Barnes, my dear friend and kindred spirit, who told me seven years ago on a brisk morning walk that I should write this book. Your enthusiasm was so contagious that it set my mind in motion to discover this new purpose in my life. No matter how slow I was to take action or stumble my way through the baby steps that followed, you continued to encourage and believe in me. Thank you for being my Earth Angel.

Deep gratitude to those who held my hand and heart with their wise counsel, whether mentally, emotionally, professionally, or spiritually—all of you were there at different times to help me become the speaker, writer, and author I am today. Thank you to Raul Quiroz, Christine Hefel, Cheryl Jones, Rebecca Easley, April Adams Pertuis, Elizabeth Gormly De Moraes, Angel Tuccy, and Lenay Vale for teaching me how to shine my light with faith, courage, and grace.

Whether you are my friend from childhood, adulthood, or from my social media family, I want to thank you for always supporting me in your own unique way. It doesn't matter if your words of encouragement were delivered in person, through my blog, or via Facebook. Every word, every hug, every pat on the back, and every share of my social media posts—these were the fuel I needed to stay the course. I couldn't be more blessed by you all.

To my second family, my hardworking fellow nurses and doctors: through all the hustle and bustle of our crazy busy shifts, ya'll managed to help me heal through my grief, not only by listening to my stories, but also by sharing your own. Thank you all for the special ways you nurtured my heart and my confidence as a nurse, a caregiver, a griever—and as a writer.

Special thanks to each and every one of my wonderful family members who sincerely supported my idea of writing this memoir. From the beginning, I have felt every ounce of your love and prayers that have gotten me to this point. How blessed I've been to have you all as part of my history, my heart, and my life. I will forever be grate-ful for the comforting and supportive ways you tended to me during the highs and lows of my writing journey.

To the ones who egged me on with my prestigious title of Tag-Along Buzzard—my brother, Mark, and my sister, Monica: there wasn't a chapter I wrote that didn't bring about a special memory of each of you. I love you both so much. Thank you for being open and respect-ing my wish to write my story. I hope this book makes you proud and serves as a reminder that no matter what we've endured as a family, we always had and will have our love, our faith, and each other to see us through.

To my beautiful children, Natalie, Nathan, Samuel, and Daniel: little did you all know that one of the main reasons your mom was so determined to break through the many barriers of her self-doubt with writing this book was to show you that with God, anything is pos-sible. I will forever appreciate and cherish all the fun and considerate ways each of you cheered me on with your handmade posters, hugs, and "You can do it, Mom" com-ments throughout the entire process. I love you all with my heart and soul.

As always, I save the biggest and best thank yous for last.

To my husband, Mike Lackey: I would thank you a thousand times if I could. From the moment I mentioned my dream of becoming an author, you never doubted me once, and you reassured me that you would be with me every step of the way. And you were. Anytime I'd lose my mojo (which was more than I'd like to admit), you revved me up with your vote of confidence, your hugs, and your quick-witted humor. You instantly became my tech guy, taking care of the computer glitches and all my user errors, even during the most inconvenient of times. And whenever this project of mine needed some extra funding, you always stepped in and worked a few extra shifts to make ends meet. Not to mention the many days and weekends when you had to fly solo with the kids while I was at the library writing away.

I know it isn't always easy being married to a busy, overthinking dreamer like me, but somehow you manage to make it look effortless. I will forever see this book as a true reflection of all the love and sacrifice you put into helping make my dream a reality. I love you with my whole heart and soul, and I will remain eternally grateful to God for allowing me to have such a wonderful husband as you.

With deep gratitude, I am proud to say that I am the woman I am today because of my beloved parents, Robert and Sandra Lozano. From the time I was a little girl to adulthood, both of you taught me the importance of true grit, hard work, unconditional love, and faith in God as a way to get through every aspect of life—including writing this book. I'm so grateful that I carry within me pieces of your spirits that have allowed me to feel every ounce of your love. I love and miss you, Mom and Dad. Thank you both for the heavenly kudos and hellos that have kept me going. You sure know how to make your baby girl feel better. I hope this book makes you proud.

And lastly, I want to give all the glory to God. I didn't think I had it in me to write a book, but through His son, Jesus, and the Holy Spirit, Mother Mary, and all my angels who rallied around me, my prayers were answered, and I was given the strength to endure any pain or setback of retelling my story and reliving my grief; for writer's block, perfectionism, and my old limited self-beliefs that left me paralyzed. Every time I think about how far I've come in my life and in my writing journey, I can't help but tear up as I acknowledge the fact that all of it was by the grace of God and his heavenly team. I am blessed.

About the Author

MARLA LACKEY is a nurse, author, blogger, speaker, and former caregiver to her beloved parents. Marla uses her soulful energy and personal stories to offer hope and inspiration to caregivers and grievers to find the blessings in the midst of their own painful journeys. .

Marla also speaks to healthcare professionals on the topic of mindfulness in healthcare and delivers helpful tips and stories of her personal and professional life, encouraging and inspiring her colleagues to connect with their patients while working and multitasking in a stressful environment.

Marla resides in Texas with her husband and four adult children. For more information, connect with her in the following ways:

Website: www.faithandlipstick.com
Facebook: @FaithAndLipstick
Instagram: @marlalackey

Made in the USA
Coppell, TX
30 November 2020